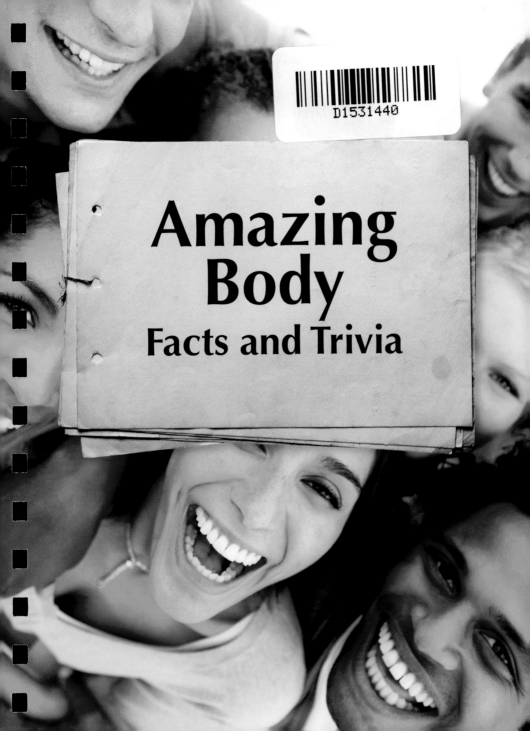

Amazing
Body
Facts and Trivia

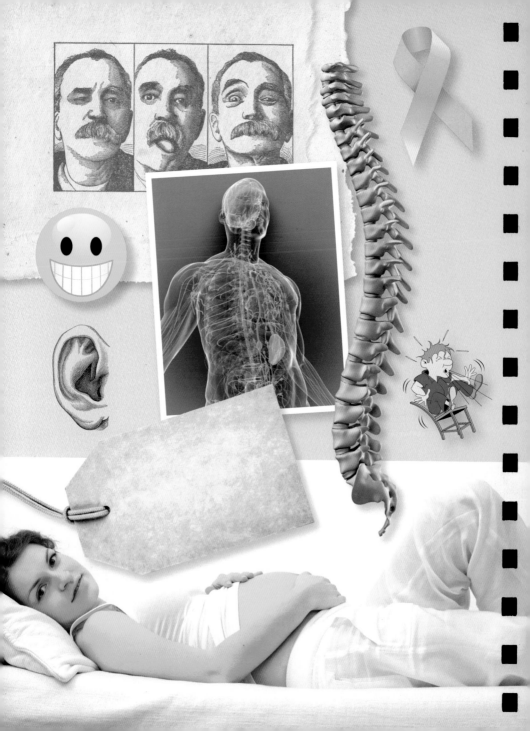

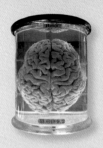

Amazing Body
Facts and Trivia

Jack Challoner

CHARTWELL
BOOKS, INC.

A QUARTO BOOK

Published in 2011 by
Chartwell Books, Inc.
A division of Book Sales, Inc.
276 Fifth Avenue Suite 206
New York, New York 10001
USA

Copyright © 2011 Quarto Inc.

ISBN-13: 978-0-7858-2743-6

Conceived, designed,
and produced by
Quarto Publishing plc
The Old Brewery
6 Blundell Street
London N7 9BH

QUA: BOFT

Design: Schermuly Design Co.
Editor: Cathy Meeus
Proofreader: Lynn Bresler
Indexer: Joan Dearnley
Art director: Caroline Guest

Creative director: Moira Clinch
Publisher: Paul Carslake

Color separation by Modern Age
Repro House Ltd, Hong Kong
Printed by Midas Printing
International Ltd, China

This book is not intended to
give medical advice; any health
concerns/decisions should be
directed to healthcare
professionals.

Contents

The contents of this book are completely random, so that each time you open it, you will discover an amazing variety of facts and trivia about the human body. If you wish to locate a particular category of information however this contents list is organized into topics. There is also an index on pages 187–192.

Introduction

**Delve into this richly illustrated book to find
a treasure trove of information about … you.**

Every human being who has ever lived spent about half
an hour as a single cell—a fertilized egg. After about
nine months of continuous cell divisions, that single
fertilized egg cell became a baby, ready to face the
world; by then, it was made of around 2 trillion cells in
more than 200 different varieties. The instructions that
tell a fertilized egg how to divide are carried in DNA—
nearly 10 feet (3 m) of it, coiled very tightly. The entire
length of DNA is then copied to every new cell. The
process of cell division continues into adulthood—the
average adult consists of around 100 trillion cells—and
cells are constantly dying and being replaced, at the rate
of about a million every second.

Every human body is an incredibly complex machine.
This book is a celebration of that machine; it is filled
with facts and explanations from anatomy, physiology,
medicine, history, and mythology. There are countless
web pages that contain lists of supposed facts about
the human body, but in most cases they are badly

explained if they are explained at all—and most have not been checked for accuracy. This book aims to set the record straight, with clear explanations and reliable facts; and it challenges many urban myths about the body—some of which are sustained by those web pages filled with "facts."

The heart of the book is an exciting jumble of facts, figures, stories, and statistics. It has an entirely random organization, so it is perfect for browsing through and stumbling upon unexpected nuggets of fascinating information, strange stories, and practical tips. But while it is delightfully unstructured, this book also boasts a helpful index that allows the reader to find information by looking up a body part or a particular theme.

The human body has inspired poets, artists, and scientists to produce remarkable work—and some of the most remarkable is laid bare in this book, which will give you a deeper understanding of your physical self, and a new appreciation of what a marvel you are. Your body is amazing—and the superlatives, uncountable numbers, lists, explanations, and anecdotes contained in this book will remind you of that.

Coconuts tried in vein

In 1999, doctors in the Solomon Islands administered coconut water as a substitute for intravenous saline solution: they gave it to a stroke patient who was too ill to drink or use a nasal tube, and the treatment was successful. This emergency technique was discovered by the British and Japanese during World War II, when it saved many lives.

Intravenous drip

The inconvenient rumbling sound made by the movement of gas and fluids in the stomach and intestines is scientifically known as "borborygmus."

INFLAMMATION OVERLOAD

One of the body's responses to damage or infection is called inflammation, which produces features such as redness, warmth, swelling, and pain in the affected area. The names of medical conditions involving inflammation have the suffix "-itis." Appendicitis, for example, is the term for inflammation of the appendix. Other inflammations include:

- Rhinitis (nasal lining)
- Hepatitis (liver)
- Dermatitis (skin)
- Tonsillitis (tonsils)
- Laryngitis (larynx)
- Arthritis (joints)
- Sinusitis (sinuses)
- Bronchitis (bronchioles—the tubes that lead to the lungs)
- Vasculitis (blood vessels)
- Encephalitis (brain)
- Meningitis (meninges—the membranes around the brain)
- Colitis (colon)
- Conjunctivitis (conjunctiva)
- Phlebitis (veins)
- Gingivitis (gums)
- Mastitis (breast tissue)
- Cystitis (urinary tract)
- Myelitis (spinal cord)
- Retinitis (retina)

HAIRY WORDS
The Albanian language has 27 different words for "mustache" and another 27 different words for "eyebrow."

OUT-OF-DATE BODY PARTS

We all have various "vestigial" parts of the body—things that evolution has rendered unimportant and functionless, but that still exist:

♥ **Appendix:** Part of the cecum, which connects the small and large intestines, the appendix would have helped our ancestors digest grasses.

♥ **Wisdom teeth:** Large molars that grow in some adults, and that would once have helped grind down grasses.

♥ **Coccyx:** A "tailbone" at the base of the spine that would have helped our ancestors with balance.

♥ **Ear muscles:** Largely nonfunctioning, these muscles would have helped turn our ears to sense danger.

♥ **Goosebumps:** The raising of hair follicles, which would have helped trap a layer of air next to the skin in our furry ancestors.

Vitruvian Man

In 1490, Italian polymath Leonardo da Vinci completed a drawing entitled *Vitruvian Man*. It was an attempt to show the beautiful proportions in the human body and was based on observations by the 1st century BCE Roman architect and engineer Vitruvius.

In the notes accompanying his drawing, da Vinci wrote:

❝ Vitruvius, the architect, says in his work on architecture that the measurements of the human body are distributed by Nature as follows: that is that 4 fingers make 1 palm, and 4 palms make 1 foot, 6 palms make 1 cubit; 4 cubits make a man's height. And 4 cubits make one pace and 24 palms make a man; and these measures he used in his buildings. If you open your legs so much as to decrease your height 1/14 and spread and raise your arms till your middle fingers touch the level of the top of your head you must know that the center of the outspread limbs will be in the navel and the space between the legs will be an equilateral triangle. The length of a man's outspread arms is equal to his height.

From the roots of the hair to the bottom of the chin is the tenth of a man's height; from the bottom of the chin to the top of his head is one-eighth of his height; from the top of the breast to the top of his head will be one-sixth of a man. From the top of the breast to the roots of the hair will be the seventh part of the whole man. From the nipples to the top of the head will be the fourth part of a man. The greatest width of the shoulders contains in itself the fourth part of the man. From the elbow to the tip of the hand will be the fifth part of a man; and from the elbow to the angle of the armpit will be the eighth part of the man. The whole hand will be the tenth part of the man; the beginning of the genitals marks the middle of the man. The foot is the seventh part of the man. From the sole of the foot to below the knee will be the fourth part of the man. From below the knee to the beginning of the genitals will be fourth part of the man. The distance from the bottom of the chin to the nose and from the roots of the hair to the eyebrows is, in each case, the same, and like the ear, a third of the face. ❞

About 8% of your body weight is made up by blood. Women have an average of 9½ pints (4.5 liters), men 10½ pints (5 liters).

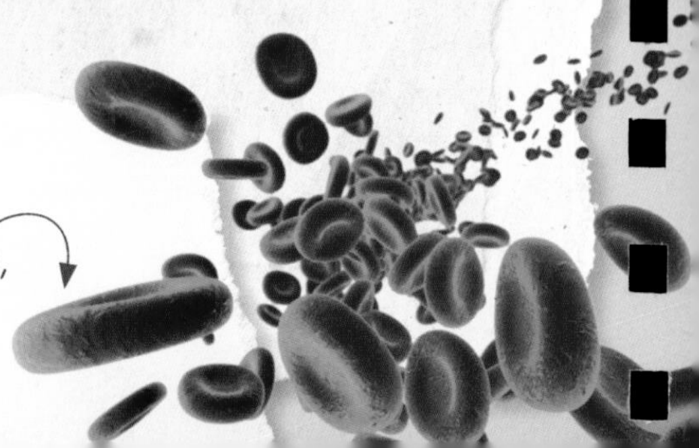

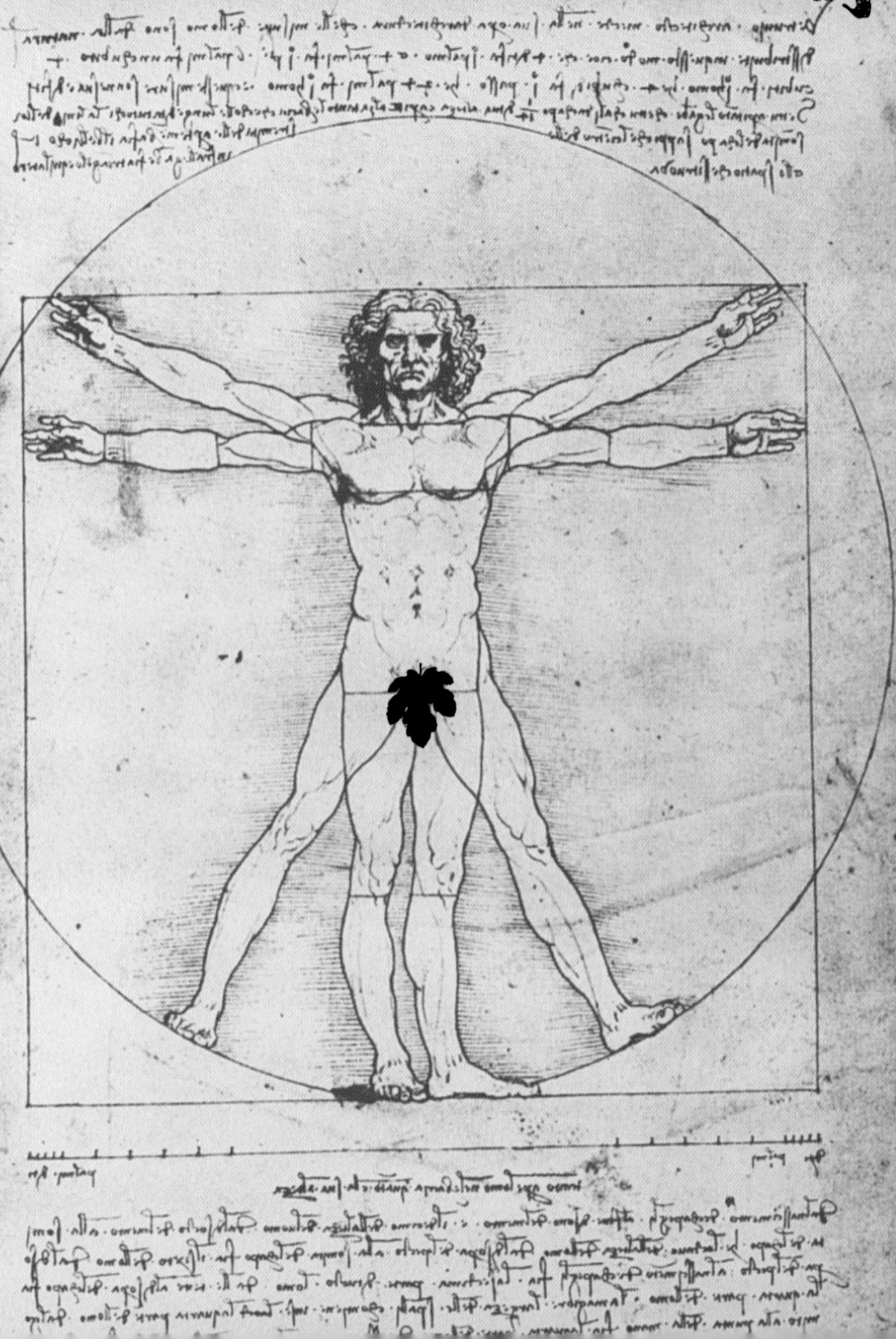

There are more bacteria in your intestines right now than all the people who have ever lived (don't worry, most of them are good for you).

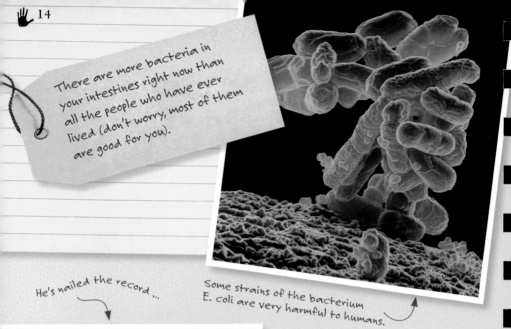

He's nailed the record ...

Some strains of the bacterium E. coli are very harmful to humans.

Fingernails

Melvin Boothe (left), from Pontiac, Michigan, had the longest fingernails ever recorded. A few months before his death in 2009, they had a total length of 32 feet 3.8 inches (9.85 m), and an average length of about 39 inches (99 cm).

Lee Redmond, from Salt Lake City, Utah, held the female record for the longest fingernails ever recorded—in 2008 their total length was 28 feet 4½ inches (8.65 m), with an average length of about 34 inches (86 cm).

Sridhar Chillal, from Pune, India, holds the record for the longest fingernails on one hand, at 20 feet 2 inches (6.15 m), with an average length of 48 inches (122 cm).

Third eye

For centuries, mystics have considered the pineal gland in the brain as a "third eye" that is able to see beyond space and time and that somehow acts as a link between the physical and spiritual worlds. In a sense, the pineal gland really is a third eye: it receives information about ambient light directly from the eye, and this information helps the gland to regulate our sleep patterns.

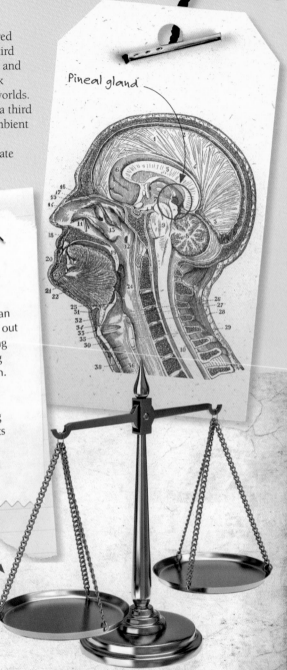

Pineal gland

THE WEIGHT OF A SOUL?

According to a bizarre experiment carried out in 1907, the body loses an average of 0.75 ounces (21 g) at the moment of death. The American doctor Duncan MacDougall carried out the gruesome experiments by placing six people onto a sensitive weighing scale when they were close to death. In 1911, MacDougall carried out another experiment, in which he tried to photograph the soul—using X-rays. Neither of these experiments has been replicated.

A 1907 experiment suggested that the soul is separate from the body and weighs in at nearly an ounce.

MORE TO FAT THAN MEETS THE SCALES

Scientists have long known that body fat acts as a store for extra calories, and that it insulates the body and protects internal organs by absorbing the knocks and shocks of everyday life. But since the early 1990s, biochemists have gradually uncovered another key job that fat performs: sending signals out to the rest of the body. Fat cells do this by producing dozens of important chemical compounds—these are mostly hormones, such as leptin and estrogen, that regulate the body's functions and "signaling proteins" called adipokines that communicate with the immune system.

Help, help, I'm being squeezed!

Jeanne Calment aged 20

Jeanne Calment aged 119

VERY OLD
The person with the longest (confirmed) lifetime was Jeanne Calment, who lived to 122 years and 164 days. She was born in Arles, France, on February 21, 1875 and died on August 4, 1997.

Bloody kidneys

Your kidneys receive about a quarter of all the blood your heart pumps: about 3.2 pints (1.5 liters) per minute in an average-sized man (a little less in a woman).

What? I've got a really bad cough!

CHOC MEDICINE

Theobromine, a natural compound found in abundance in chocolate, is more effective than codeine, the active ingredient in over-the-counter cough medicines, as a remedy for persistent coughs, U.K. researchers have revealed.

My median preoptic nucleus made me fall asleep—now how do I wake up?

Sleeper cells

Neuroscientists have tried for many years to figure out how the brain coordinates its transition from wakefulness to sleep. In 2008, scientists at the University of California, Los Angeles, discovered that a small number of neurons in part of the brain called the "median preoptic nucleus" become active 20 seconds before the onset of sleep. The median preoptic nucleus is one area of the hypothalamus, a part of the brain involved in many of the body's basic functions.

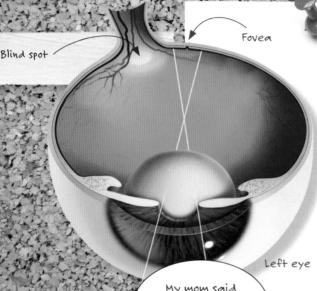

Blind spot

Fovea

Left eye

Crystal clear

You can see clearly only in the very center of your vision, the part that corresponds to the fovea (the area of the retina with the highest concentration of light-sensitive cells). When you view a scene, your brain makes your eyes scan around the central area so that it can present you with a clear "picture" of the outside world.

My mom said I'd never measure up to much.

GETTING THE MEASURE OF CRIMINALS

In 1883, French police officer Alphonse Bertillon devised a system for identifying individuals based on measurements of their bodies. He worked out that a list of eleven measurements would provide a unique profile of a person. His system, known as anthropometry, was quickly adopted by police forces in several countries. Within a few years, however, the rather simpler system of fingerprinting replaced it.

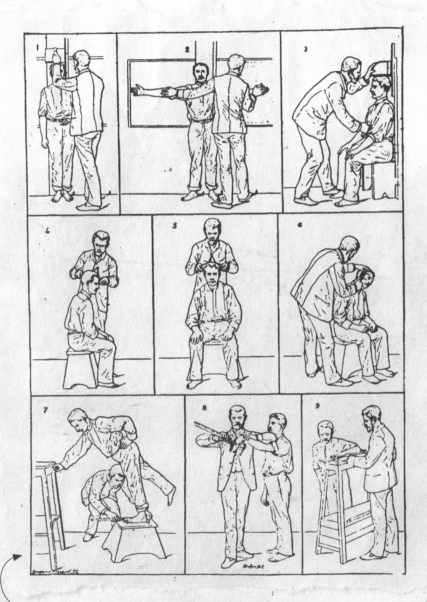

Here are nine of Alphonse Bertillon's measurements.

Plumping up

The number of fat cells (adipocytes) in your fatty tissues remains largely unchanged after adolescence. If you put on weight, it is the amount of fat stored in each fat cell, and not the number of fat cells, that increases.

STIFF

Rigor mortis—the stiffening of the body—sets in about two hours after death. It is caused by a chain of chemical reactions that starts as the body runs out of oxygen. The result of the reactions is that the muscles contract but do not relax again, as they would normally do. Rigor mortis begins all over the body at the same time, but it affects smaller muscles first. After typically about ten hours, the entire body is stiff, and it remains so until about 36 hours later, when the muscles soften as the body begins the slow process of decomposition.

I'm bored stiff!

Dying peacefully makes rigor mortis begin slowly; dying while very active makes it begin quickly.

The damage worms can do

When certain species of tiny nematode worms (roundworms), especially *Wuchereria bancrofti*, infect the lymphatic system, they can cause a painful, unsightly swelling of lower parts of the body known as elephantiasis. The condition is often mistakenly heard as "elephantitis."

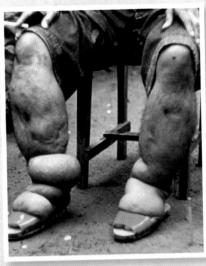

Elephantiasis of the legs caused by blockage of the lymphatic system due to infection by nematode worms.

HOW FAST DO THEY GROW?

Uncut and unbitten, your fingernails would be 1 inch (2.5 cm) longer every eight months. The exact rate depends upon age, sex, and season: growth is faster in younger people, in males, and during summer months.

Egyptian arm

The cubit is the earliest known unit of length and was in use for centuries and in several countries. It was originally based upon the length of the forearm. The ancient Egyptian cubit was around 22½ inches (52 cm) long, and consisted of 7 "palms" of 4 "digits" each.

1 cubit

Overweight, underweight—or somewhere in between?

Body mass index (BMI) is the most common way of determining if someone's weight is in the healthy range for their height. The World Health Organization uses BMI in working out its statistics on obesity. A person's BMI is calculated by dividing their mass by the square of their height. To do this using either imperial or metric units, use one of the following equations:

BMI = mass (lb) ÷ height in inches ÷ height in inches × 703

BMI = mass (kg) ÷ height in m ÷ height in m

You are in the healthy range—neither underweight nor overweight—if your BMI is between 18.5 and 24.9.

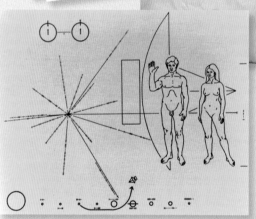

Pioneer 10's famed plaque features a design engraved into a gold-anodized aluminum plate, 6 by 9 inches (152 by 229 mm), attached to the spacecraft's antenna support struts to help shield it from erosion by interstellar dust.

One giant leap for the human body

In 1972, the National Aeronautics and Space Administration (NASA) in the U.S.A. launched into space the first of two aluminum plaques showing, among other things, the figures of a human male and female body, a silhouette of the spacecraft, and a schematic diagram of the Solar System. The plaque was fixed to the space probe *Pioneer 10*. A year later, an identical plaque was fixed to its sister craft, *Pioneer 11*.

A NOSE BY ANY OTHER NAME WOULD SMELL ...

- **Latin**: nãsus
- **Old English**: nosu
- **Afrikaans**: neus
- **German**: Nase
- **Swedish**: näsa
- **Polish**: nos
- **Portuguese**: nariz
- **Estonian**: nina
- **Hungarian**: orr
- **Swahili**: pua
- **Malay**: hidung
- **Slang:** conk, hooter, neb, schnoz, schnozzle, snout.

Nice schnoz

A typical square inch of skin sheds around 650,000 particles of dead skin per hour—that debris makes up 80% of household dust.

Making the body perfect?

More than 10 million cosmetic "enhancements" are performed each year in the U.S.A. alone. Here are just a few of the procedures that people undertake. All of them have risks, some more than others:

Mammoplasty: Surgeon adds (breast enhancement) or removes (breast reduction) material to the breasts, or removes skin above the breast (breast lift).

Abdominoplasty: Surgeon removes a little fat and excess skin from the abdomen, to firm up the tummy. Also known as a "tummy tuck."

Penis enlargement: Surgeon increases the length or the girth of the penis, most commonly by injecting or implanting natural or synthetic material into it.

Liposuction: Surgeon removes excess fatty tissue, typically from thighs, tummy or buttocks (sometimes also carried out for noncosmetic reasons).

Thigh lift: Surgeon removes excess, sagging skin from the inner thigh.

Laser hair removal: Practitioner uses a laser to selectively destroy melanin in hair follicles; melanin is the pigment that gives skin and hair its color.

A developing fetus typically begins to hear during the eighteenth week of pregnancy, at which time they may be startled by loud sounds.

Dermabrasion:
Practitioner uses a rapidly spinning abrasive wheel to remove the upper layers of skin on the face, encouraging the production of new skin.

Chemical peel: Practitioner applies a chemical solution to the face that causes the outer layers of skin to blister and peel, so that they are replaced by new skin.

Eyelid surgery: Surgeon removes excess skin, muscle, or fat from around the eye, to improve the appearance of droopy eyelids.

Collagen injection: Practitioner injects collagen (typically sourced from a cow) under the skin of the face, to get rid of wrinkles or reduce the appearance of scars.

Otoplasty: Surgeon changes the appearance of the ears, most commonly by sculpting the cartilage and pulling the ears closer to the head by tying them with a suture.

Botox injection: Practitioner injects a toxic bacterial protein called botulinum toxin into the face—typically around the eye—to paralyze the muscles, reducing wrinkles.

Rhinoplasty: Surgeon reshapes the nose, by sculpting the bone and cartilage inside.

Lip augmentation: Practitioner injects one of several natural and synthetic materials into the lips, to increase their "fullness."

Facelift: Surgeon removes fat, tightens muscular tissue, and rewraps skin around the face and neck, to reduce sagging.

The body's single currency

One of the most crucial chemical reactions in your body is the conversion of adenosine diphosphate (ADP) into adenosine triphosphate (ATP). It may sound vague, geeky, and complex, but this reaction is absolutely central to how your body functions—and it is happening continuously in every cell in your body. ATP is a supercharged carrier of chemical energy, thanks to the addition of a phosphate group to ADP. The phosphate groups are the groups of yellow (phosphor) and red (oxygen) atoms at the end of the molecules shown below.

The energy is typically produced by cellular respiration, a process that involves oxygen in your body cells reacting with glucose, a sugar derived from food. The energy is used for carrying out all of the body's vital housekeeping tasks: from making new skin to fighting disease, to making nerve cells fire to making muscle cells contract, the list is endless. Once an ATP molecule gives up its extra energy, it returns to its original state, as ADP. Around ten million ATP molecules are recycled in this way every second in each working muscle cell.

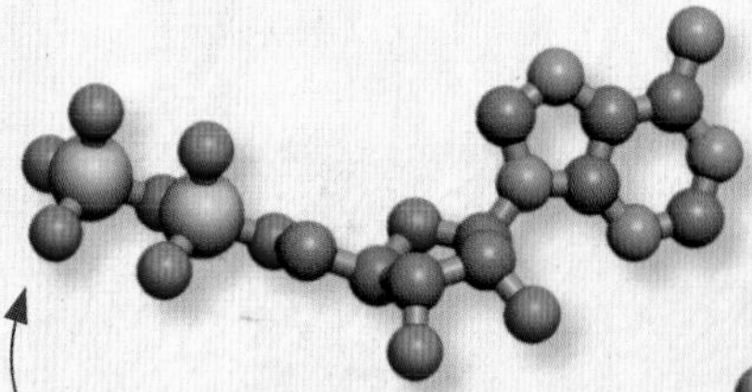

Adenosine diphosphate (ADP)

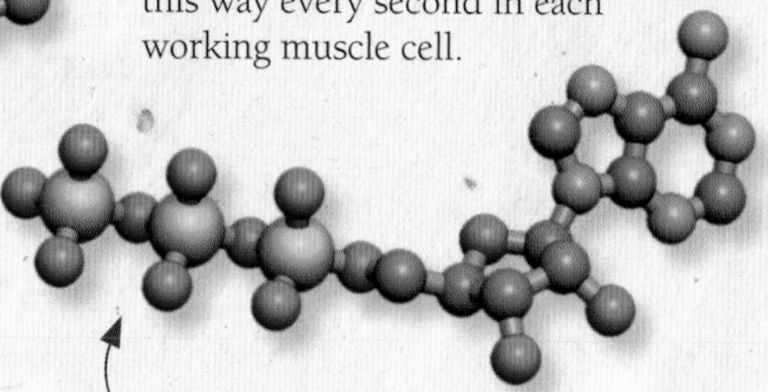

Adenosine triphosphate (ATP)

Section through a femur, or thigh bone. The porous inside part, called cancellous bone, contains red and yellow marrow.

THE HARD FACTS

Living bones are rigid, but they are not hard or brittle. Bone marrow, blood vessels, and bone cells (osteocytes) account for 20 percent of the mass of a living bone—the rest is mostly long fibers of collagen, interspersed with the mineral "carbonated hydroxylapatite," a form of calcium phosphate. This bone mineral makes up about half of the dry weight of a bone and is what gives dry bones their white color.

Cousin chimp

Our closest living relative is the chimpanzee. Both humans and chimpanzees are from the family Hominidae, as are gorillas and orangutans. The genomes of humans and chimps are very similar—about 98 percent of our genes are common. Both species originated from a common ancestor that looked like a lemur and lived around seven million years ago. But just how different—and how similar—are we?

HUMANS	CHIMPANZEES
Walk on two legs (bipedal)	Mostly walk on all fours, using their knuckles
Eat meat and vegetables (omnivorous)	Eat meat and vegetables (omnivorous)
Use sophisticated language	Use basic language
Thumb separate from fingers, allowing a grip (opposable thumb)	Thumb separate from fingers, allowing a grip (opposable thumb)
No external tail (just a remnant, the coccyx)	No external tail (just a remnant, the coccyx)
Mostly "naked," with hair concentrated in certain places	Hairy all over
Average brain volume 73 cubic inches (1,200 cubic cm)	Average brain volume 21 cubic inches (350 cubic cm)
Arm span equivalent to height	Arm span greater than height
Tall forehead, to accommodate larger frontal lobe in the brain	Small forehead
No opposable big toe	Opposable big toe—chimps can grip with their feet
32 teeth	32 teeth
Small pointed teeth (canines)	Large pointed teeth (canines)
Male adults grow to average 6 feet (1.8 m)	Male adults grow to average 4 feet (1.2 m)
Chromosomes: 46 (23 pairs)	Chromosomes: 48 (24 pairs)
Thin tooth enamel	Thick tooth enamel
Teeth move in a crushing action	Teeth move in a grinding action
Hole in the base of the skull (foramen magnum) is at the center of of the head	Hole in the base of the skull (foramen magnum) is toward the rear of the head
Shinbone (tibia) is thick and straight	Shinbone (tibia) is thin and angled

YOUR BODY NEEDS ...

... magnesium

The metallic element magnesium is vital to many important body functions: it is involved in more than 300 biochemical reactions and is present in every cell of your body. A deficiency of magnesium may result in general fatigue, muscle weakness, a compromised immune system, high blood pressure, and hyperactivity. The recommended daily intake of magnesium is 400 mg. Good sources of this important mineral include green vegetables, halibut, nuts, seeds, beans, and baked potato.

Magnesium
crystals

Broccoli contains
magnesium

HOLE IN THE HEART

All babies are born with a hole in the heart. It is called the foramen ovale, and it allows most of the baby's blood to bypass the baby's lungs. The foramen ovale forms in the fourth week of gestation and closes over in the first few weeks after birth.

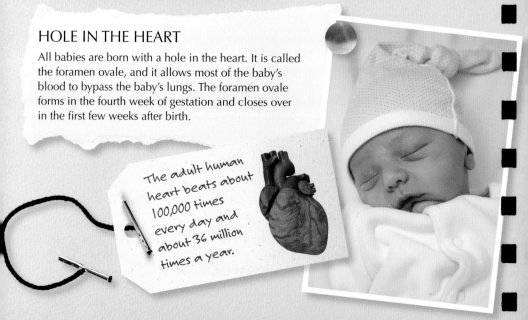

The adult human heart beats about 100,000 times every day and about 36 million times a year.

Wow! This is supertasty.

THE B LISTERS

There is a complex of eight B vitamins altogether, all soluble in water and all vital. Vitamin B1 was the first vitamin to be isolated, after scientists had noted that a chemical present in rice bran prevented beriberi, a disease of the nervous system. The word "vitamin" derives from *vita* (Latin for "life") and "amine" (the class of chemicals).

Foods rich in the B vitamins include: unrefined (whole-grain) cereals, liver, beef, tuna, turkey, Brazil nuts, bananas, potatoes, avocados, peas, and beans.

Vitamin B_1 (thiamine, isolated 1910)

Vitamin B_2 (riboflavin, 1920)

Vitamin B_3 (niacin, discovered 1936)

Vitamin B_5 (pantothenic acid, 1931)

Vitamin B_6 (pyridoxine, 1934)

Vitamin B_7 (biotin, 1931)

Vitamin B_9 (folic acid, 1941)

Vitamin B_{12} (cobalamin, 1926)

Nearly two-thirds of the dry weight of feces is composed of dead gut bacteria.

Supertasters versus supertaskers

In 1990, American taste researcher Linda Bartoshuk coined the term "supertaster" to describe those people who have a larger than normal number of taste buds (more than 10,000 compared to the normal 4,000 or so). Supertasters are particularly sensitive to flavor. There are certain foods they typically do not like, including broccoli, Brussels sprouts, fizzy drinks, coffee, and artificial sweeteners. About 25 percent of people are supertasters; you are slightly more likely to be a supertaster if you are female and if you are from African or Asian descent.

In 2010, American neuroscientist Jason Watson coined the term "supertasker" to describe those people whose brains are able to focus their attention on two or more things at once. Research has shown time and time again that most people can focus on only one complex task at a time—so if they are speaking on a mobile phone while driving, one of the tasks must suffer. Watson found that 2.5 percent of people are supertaskers.

Too much salt!

High blood pressure (hypertension) is a big problem in modern societies: it increases the risk of a stroke and heart attack. One of its major causes is high levels of salt in the diet. Salt, or sodium chloride (NaCl), is an essential part of your diet, but too much causes your body to retain more fluid, which in turn increases the pressure on your blood vessels, raising your blood pressure level.

Nutrition experts in various countries make slightly different recommendations about the amount of salt we should have in our diets—and how much is too much. In most cases, they advise consuming not more than 5-6 g (about a teaspoonful) of salt per day. In some cases, they use the amount of sodium present as the reference point, and some food labels reflect this—6 g (6,000 mg) of salt contains 2,400 mg of sodium. (There are 1,000 mg of sodium in 2,500 mg of salt, so to find the mass of sodium present in a certain amount of salt, just divide by 2.5.)

PLENTIFUL SUPPORT

For every neuron in the brain that actually receives and transmits signals, there are several glial cells, which physically support the neurons and supply them with nutrients.

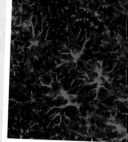

The most common type of glial cell are the star-shaped astrocytes, stained red here against a darker background.

Aloe vera

The sap of the succulent plant aloe vera has been widely used in herbal medicine for at least 3,600 years. Today, it is a popular ingredient in many cosmetics and alternative remedies. Scientific studies show that it contains antibacterial and antifungal agents that can be effective against minor skin infections. A 2009 review of scientific studies about aloe vera concluded that it can be an effective treatment for frostbite and burns, can speed the healing of wounds, and can help to reduce inflammation.

Needles and pins

The technical term for the tingling sensation commonly referred to as "pins and needles" is paresthesia.

In the late stages of pregnancy, a woman's blood volume increases by about 50%.

Gabriele Falloppio

Bartolomeo Eustachi

NAME THAT TUBE …

The fallopian tubes, which guide eggs from a female's ovaries to her uterus, are named after the 16th-century Italian anatomist and doctor Gabriele Falloppio.

The eustachian tubes, which connect the middle ears and the throat and allow for pressure in the ears to equalize when you swallow, are named after the 16th-century Italian anatomist Bartolomeo Eustachi.

Nictating membrane half closed

No need for another eyelid

The small fold of moist skin at the corner of your eye nearest to your nose is called the plica semilunaris. It is a vestigial organ: a hangover from our very distant, prehuman ancestors, for whom it acted as a "third eyelid" that swept across the eye to protect and moisten it even while the main eyelids remained open. Birds and reptiles and some mammals still have a working third eyelid—it is called a nictating membrane.

Plica semilunaris

The term "Siamese twins" originated with the 19th-century conjoined twins Chang and Eng Bunker, who lived in Thailand, which was known as "Siam" at the time.

Chang and Eng Bunker, circa 1865.

Unwanted invaders

Infectious diseases are caused by microorganisms, such as bacteria and
viruses, invading the body. In some cases, the symptoms of the illness
are actually the body's response to the invasion of the organisms.
In other cases, they are the result of toxins released by the organisms.

PATHOGEN	DESCRIPTION	EXAMPLE DISEASES
BACTERIUM	A single-celled organism with no nucleus.	Tuberculosis (TB), pertussis (whooping cough), cholera, leprosy, Lyme disease, chlamydia, typhoid. Pneumonia and meningitis may also be viral.
VIRUS	A tiny object made of genetic material (DNA or RNA) with a protein "coat."	AIDS (acquired immune deficiency syndrome), influenza ('flu), herpes, measles, mumps. Pneumonia and meningitis may also be bacterial.
PROTIST	Microscopic organism whose cells have a nucleus. Protozoa are single-celled protists.	Malaria, sleeping sickness, amebic dysentery, giardiasis.
MICROSCOPIC FUNGI (yeasts and molds)	The cells of these organisms have a nucleus that has features of both plant and animal nuclei.	Candidiasis (thrush), athlete's foot, ringworm, California disease.
PRION	Tiny particle similar to a virus but made almost entirely of protein.	Creutzfeldt–Jakob disease (CJD), kuru, fatal familial insomnia.
WORM	Parasitic worms are called helminths. There are three kinds: flatworms, tapeworms, and flukes.	Bilharzia (schistosomiasis), river blindness (onchocerciasis), trichuriasis (coccidioidomycosis).

Eye see

The lining of the back of your eye is called the retina. Light passing through your eye's lens falls on the retina and passes through eight of its layers before hitting the ninth, light-sensitive layer. This contains about 90 million rod cells (sensitive only to light intensity) and about 4.5 million cone cells (sensitive to color).

Colored scanning electron micrograph (SEM) of a section through a human retina

Cone cells (yellow)

Surface layer (brown)

Optical ganglion cells (red)

Rod cells (white)

I tense my levator labii superioris alaeque nasi muscle at you!

The muscle with the longest name is the levator labii superioris alaeque nasi muscle. It lifts the upper lip in a snarl.

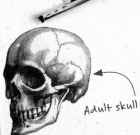

Adult skull

Babies' skulls are composed of about 400 small bony parts, which gradually fuse to give the 22 bones of the adult skull.

Mmmmm ... Donuts!

Not so sweet

Eating too much sugar may do more than make you put on weight or make you feel sick. Inside your body, some sugar molecules combine chemically with fats and protein molecules to form compounds called advanced glycation endproducts (AGEs). Some of these AGEs are insidious molecules that cause damage inside cells and play a part in age-related diseases such as Alzheimer's disease.

MILKY WORDS

♥ **Lactogenesis:** The production of milk in the mammary glands, in the breasts.

♥ **Lactation:** The secretion of milk, from the mammary glands.

♥ **Galactagogue:** Any substance that promotes lactation; examples include asparagus and brewer's yeast.

♥ **Lactifuge:** Any substance that reduces or stops the production of milk.

♥ **Galactorrhea:** The secretion of milk, from the breasts, in a spontaneous fashion, not by a new mother. Even some babies do this. Also known as nipple discharge.

♥ **Lactose:** $C_{12}H_{22}O_{11}$, a sugar that is present in milk.

♥ **Lactiferous:** Conveying milk; the lactiferous glands carry milk from the mammary glands to the nipples.

♥ **Prolactin:** A hormone that stimulates the production of milk.

♥ **Lactase:** An enzyme that helps you digest milk; absence of this enzyme makes you lactose intolerant.

♥ **Lactoprotein:** Any protein found in milk.

The normal internal body temperature is 98.6°F (37.0°C). Normal temperature measurement taken under the tongue is slightly lower.

Cranial nerves

Twelve pairs of nerves, the cranial nerves, connect
directly to the brain, rather than via the spinal cord.

NERVE PAIR	WHAT THEY DO
Olfactory nerves	Transmit information about smells from nerve endings in the upper part of the nasal cavity to the olfactory bulb at the base of the brain.
Optic nerves	Carry visual information directly from the retinas of the eyes to the brain.
Oculomotor nerves	Control most of the muscles of the eyes, including keeping the eyelids open and widening and constricting the pupils.
Trochlear nerves	Control the fine movements of the eyeballs and are involved in tracking and fixating on an object.
Trigeminal nerves	Carry sensory information from the face and also activate muscles responsible for chewing, biting, and swallowing.
Abducens nerves	Each nerve controls just one muscle, the lateral rectus muscle, which turns the eyeball from side to side.
Facial nerves	Activate the muscles that create facial expressions; another branch brings taste information from the front two-thirds of the tongue and palate. They are also involved in the blink reflex.
Vestibulocochlear nerves	Connect the ears to the brain, carrying sound and balance information from the inner ear.
Glossopharyngeal nerves	Perform many functions, including carrying taste information from the rear one-third of the tongue, carrying sensory information from the tonsils, and controlling a muscle that lifts the larynx (voice box) and widens the throat during swallowing.
Vagus nerves	Control muscles in the throat, larynx, lungs, heart, esophagus, and intestines. They are responsible for controlling heart rate, sweating, and speech. They also bring information from the ear, tongue, pharynx, and larynx.
Accessory nerves	Control the muscles of the neck; they are, for example, responsible for lifting the shoulders and rotating the head.
Hypoglossal nerves	Control the muscles of the tongue.

Eat less, drink red wine, live longer—but ask the doc first!

Severe calorie restriction—consuming just enough calories to survive—increases well-being and extends longevity in a wide range of living things. One of the reasons seems to lie in the genes. In the 1990s, researchers discovered genes that activate during scarcity or other stressful conditions to improve the body's chances of getting through the crisis. These genes seem to switch on during calorie restriction, and if they remain active, they can dramatically enhance an organism's health and extend its life. The most important are genes called sirtuin genes, in particular, the gene known as Sir2. Simply having an extra copy of this gene tends to extend an organism's life.

There is increasing evidence that calorie restriction may benefit humans. For example, blood pressure and blood cholesterol levels tend to assume ideal values, obesity is ruled out, and memory and alertness often improve. In the human genome, Sir2 is called SIRT1. A compound called resveratrol, found in red wine, has been found to increase the activity of SIRT1. NOTE: don't reduce your calorie intake dramatically without seeking medical advice—you could suffer from malnutrition, which would not be healthy. And red wine has positive effects only in moderation.

This 11-month-old baby boy has six fingers on each hand.

THE AVERAGE NUMBER OF FINGERS
Polydactyly—the rare condition of having more than the normal number of fingers or toes—raises our average number of fingers and toes to more than ten each.

WHAT IS THIS?

Answers on page 186.

Catman

STALKING CAT

American computer repair man Dennis Avner (born 1958) is generally known by the nickname "Catman"—but he prefers his Native American name, "Stalking Cat." He has undergone many cosmetic procedures, all with the aim of achieving oneness with his totem, the tiger. In fact, he holds the world record for having had the most modifications carried out on his body. Procedures he has undergone include having dentures fitted in the shape of feline fangs and steel implants inserted in his cheeks, on which to fix detachable whiskers.

Julius Caesar from the Gardens of the Tuileries in Paris.

Not Caesar

The term "cesarean section" comes from the Latin word *caedare*, meaning "to cut." It is not named after the Roman emperor Julius Caesar, who was not born by cesarean section. However, Roman author Pliny the Elder suggested that Caesar's own family name originated in the fact that one of his ancestors was indeed born by cesarean section.

Facing the facts

In the 1997 film *Face Off*, the characters played by John Travolta and Nicolas Cage undergo face transplant surgery, so that they take on each other's appearance. After the operations, each one looks exactly like the other did. In reality, the bone structure underneath the face contributes to a person's appearance, and the two would have looked quite different. The world's first full face transplant was completed in Spain in March 2010. The recipient of a donor face was a 31-year-old farmer known only as "Oscar," who was left unable to breathe, swallow, or speak following a shooting accident in 2005.

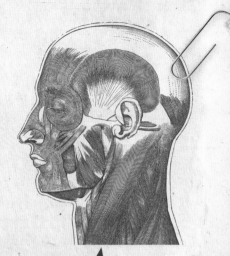

The muscles of the face are anchored to the skull.

YOUR BODY NEEDS ...

... potassium

About 95 percent of the body's potassium is stored in the fluids inside cells—the rest is dissolved in the blood. Potassium plays an important role in building proteins, in the contraction of muscles, and in the electrical activity of nerves. A deficiency of potassium (hypokalemia) is rare and is usually caused by loss of the mineral through dehydration, rather than through malnutrition, since it is a very common mineral. Good sources of potassium include fruit (particularly bananas), vegetables, bean, nuts, milk, fish, beef, chicken, and bread.

You'd have to be bananas to miss out on your potassium.

Dying to get involved in anatomical research?

Until the middle of the 19th century, most cadavers (dead bodies) used in anatomical studies were those of executed criminals. But during the 19th century, capital punishment rates went down in several countries, and the practice of body snatching became more commonplace. Most body snatchers would secretly dig up bodies soon after they had been buried—but some killed people instead. The most famous were William Burke and William Hare, who moved to Edinburgh, Scotland, from the Province of Ulster, Ireland, in 1827. Between November 1827 and October 1828, these two men committed 17 murders and sold the cadavers to an anatomy lecturer called Dr. Robert Knox. Burke was hanged in January 1829, but Hare was set free in return for giving evidence against his partner in crime.

These stones were all passed naturally by the same person.

WEE STONES

Urine, formed in the kidneys, contains dissolved minerals. Sometimes, these minerals come out of solution and form crystals, commonly called kidney stones. These crystals are normally so small that they pass easily out with the urine. If a crystal grows larger than about ¹/₁₀ inch (2.5 mm) in diameter, it can block the ureter—the tube that leads from the kidneys to the bladder. The ureter is lined with muscle, and the blockage causes the muscle to twitch in an attempt to move the crystal, which can be very painful. Kidney stones have no doubt been forming since the dawn of the human race—they form in other animals, too—but the oldest known case is nearly 7,000 years old. It was discovered in 1901 by British archaeologist Elliot Smith, inside a mummified body in El Amrah, Egypt, which was dated to 4,800 BCE.

The system of arteries that surround the brain stem and supply blood to the brain is called the circle of Willis. It is named after 17th-century English physician Thomas Willis, and it looks uncannily like a stick person.

AMINO ACIDS

Your body breaks down (catabolizes) protein molecules in your food into their constituent parts—small molecules called amino acids. These smaller molecules are used in various important ways, including providing a source of energy and acting as neurotransmitters—chemical messengers that carry information across the gaps between nerve cells. Their main job, however, is to build proteins, which are made of chains of amino acids joined together.

The amino acids involved in building proteins are shown in the list below. Some amino acids are "essential," which means they can only be obtained through your diet; your body can make the others itself.

- Alanine
- Arginine
- Asparagine
- Aspartic acid
- Cysteine
- Glutamic acid
- Glutamine
- Glycine
- Histidine (essential)
- Isoleucine (essential)
- Leucine (essential)
- Lysine (essential)
- Methionine (essential)
- Phenylalanine (essential)
- Proline
- Serine
- Threonine (essential)
- Tryptophan (essential)
- Tyrosine
- Valine (essential)

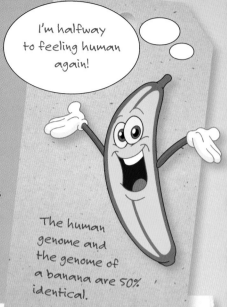

I'm halfway to feeling human again!

The human genome and the genome of a banana are 50% identical.

Going without

An initially healthy human body can survive without food for about eight weeks. The length of time a human body can survive without water depends upon the circumstances—but it is certainly no more than four or five days. We lose water through evaporation when we sweat and with each breath, and we lose water in our urine and feces. In hot conditions, a person could die from dehydration in less than a day.

Robert Wadlow on his 17th birthday with his brothers.

THEY MIGHT HAVE BEEN GIANTS

The tallest man ever recorded was an American, Robert Wadlow (1918–1940), born in Alton, Illinois. He grew to 8 feet $11\frac{1}{10}$ inches (2.72 m). The tallest woman ever recorded was Zeng Jinlian (1964–1982), born in Xiangtan, Hunan Province, China. She grew to 8 feet $1\frac{4}{5}$ inches (2.48 m). Both stood more than 5 feet (1.52 m) tall by the age of 4.

Heart of the matter

William Harvey

Until the 17th century, people believed that the blood was made in the liver and "consumed" in the body's organs, being absorbed like water used for irrigation in the fields. It was English physician William Harvey (1578–1657) who worked out that blood circulates in the body, pumping out from the heart through arteries and returning in the veins. Harvey's first clue was the valves in veins, which allow blood to flow in one direction only. Then, by cutting up living animals, he could see that the heart was a pump. Harvey's master stroke was to multiply the volume of the heart (about 2 fluid ounces, or 60 ml) by the number of times the heart pumps each day. The result was far greater than the body could ever make, proving that the blood was recycled, not absorbed.

A discovery by Italian microscopist Marcello Malphigi (1628–1684) made Harvey's cycle complete. Gazing through a powerful microscope, Malphigi discovered the capillaries: tiny blood vessels that allow flesh to be infused with blood and provide the vital connection between arteries and veins.

CLEFT AND CREASE
The vertical dividing line of the buttocks is called the intergluteal cleft; the horizontal crease at the bottom of the buttocks is called the gluteal sulcus.

Eight glasses of water

Water you talking about?

There is a common misconception, amplified and sustained by countless web pages and magazine articles, that we must drink eight glasses of water every day—and that if we don't, we risk dehydration, fatigue, and may even increase the risk of cancer. Water is certainly vital for our body's functions: every one of your cells consists mostly of water, and you lose about 3 pints (1.5 liters) on an ordinary day (much more if you do heavy exercise). But you take in more than 2 pints (1 liter) of water every day without drinking a drop—it's in your food. And if your level of hydration falls even a tiny amount below normal, your body responds by reducing the amount of water excreted, producing a strong craving: thirst. In 2004, the Institute of Medicine in the U.S.A. declared that "the vast majority of healthy people adequately meet their daily hydration needs by letting thirst be their guide."

Coffee is fluid.

Several scientific studies have debunked another myth about water intake: the idea that drinking caffeinated drinks, such as tea or coffee, will cause your body to lose more water than the volume of the drink. The studies found that caffeine has a very mild diuretic effect (makes you need to urinate)—but no more so than water alone, and certainly not enough that the body will lose more water than is in the drink itself.

There are 16 muscles in the tongue.

Mite be no problem

About half of us have thousands of tiny parasitic mites living on our faces—in particular, around our eyelashes. These usually harmless eight-legged creatures are less than 1/50 inch (0.5 mm) long. There are two species: *Demodex folliculorum*, which live in hair follicles, and *Demodex brevis*, which live in the sebaceous glands (which produce sebum, which lubricates the skin and hair).

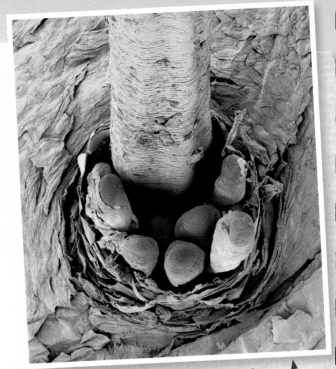

Eyelash mite tails grouped around the shaft of an eyelash where it emerges from a hair follicle.

The biggest preventable cause of death in the world has remained the same for many years: malnutrition. According to a United Nations estimate (2001), simply not having enough of the right things to eat claims about 36 million lives each year—either directly or indirectly. This represents an average of more than one death every second.

Mouthwatering mixture ...

There is more to spit than meets the eye. Spit, properly called saliva, is mostly water: 98 percent water, in fact. That makes it ideal for lubricating your food and dissolving some of the nutrients. But this vital mixture, produced by three salivary glands located around the mouth, also contains enzymes, antibiotics, and other important substances. Estimates vary on how much saliva we produce each day, but most suggest that it is about 2 pints (1 liter). Saliva production all but shuts down while you are asleep. The main constituents of saliva are ...

SUBSTANCE	FUNCTION
Water	Lubricates food to make it easier to swallow, suspends or dissolves other salivary substances, and dilutes acid produced by bacteria.
Amylase (enzyme)	Starts to break down starch into glucose, the simple sugar that is your body's main energy source.
Lingual lipase (enzyme)	Breaks down fat, but doesn't start working until it reaches the acidic conditions of the stomach.
Antibacterial enzymes, such as lysozome and lactoperoxidase	Kill bacteria
Dissolved minerals including sodium, potassium, calcium, phosphorus	No particular purpose—they are found in all bodily fluids.
Proteins	Help to build tooth enamel and aid in lubrication of food.
Opiorphin	Painkiller
Extracellular superoxide dismutase (enzyme)	Antioxidant enzyme that helps to reduce damage inside cells, by disarming a very reactive free radical called superoxide.
Millions of cells, both your own and bacterial ones	No function—these are just part of the mix.

About one in every 80,000 babies is born with the membrane of the amniotic sac (the caul) over their faces—this does no harm and in medieval times was seen as good luck.

Stop the rot

Left untreated, a human corpse decomposes. First, microbes such as bacteria begin breaking down soft tissues as they feed off them. Then, maggots do the same, only more rapidly. But under certain conditions decomposition can be slowed or even stopped. Here's how:

1. A corpse buried or enclosed shortly after death will decay more slowly, because flies cannot get to it.

2. Embalming solutions, injected into corpses by funeral directors, slow the decomposition. These liquids contain chemicals that make proteins in the soft tissues unavailable for the microbes.

3. In very cold conditions, microbes shut down and the flies' eggs do not hatch into maggots; frozen bodies can last for hundreds of years in a mummified state.

4. A body can remain well preserved for hundreds of years in a bog, due to acidic conditions and low temperatures.

5. Very dry conditions can desiccate a corpse, and the organisms that decompose the body cannot survive without water.

6. Mummification, as famously practiced by the ancient Egyptians.

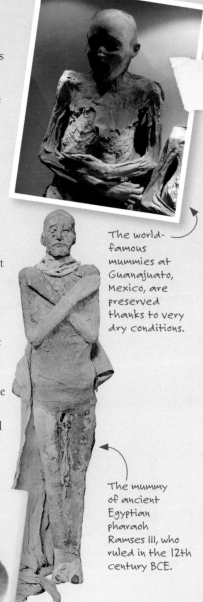

The world-famous mummies at Guanajuato, Mexico, are preserved thanks to very dry conditions.

The mummy of ancient Egyptian pharaoh Ramses III, who ruled in the 12th century BCE.

The word "muscle" comes from the Greek word "musculus," meaning "little mouse," because of the way some contracting muscles under the skin look like mice under a rug or cloth.

DON'T IT MAKE YOUR BLUE EYES BROWN

The huge range of colors of the human iris is due to differing levels of just one pigment: melanin, which also occurs in hair and skin. Melanin absorbs light, and different amounts cause different wavelengths of light to exit the iris, producing different colors. Blue-eyed people have little melanin in their irises: their color is produced by light scattering; a similar process makes the sky blue.

Brown is the most common eye color in the world—more than half of us have brown eyes.

One of the most remarkable bog mummies is Grauballe Man, discovered in Denmark in 1952. It is about 2,300 years old.

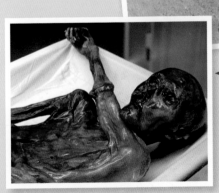

This preserved corpse, nicknamed Ötzi the Iceman, was discovered in 1991 in a glacier near the border between Austria and Italy. Its age is estimated at 5,300 years.

Ringing in your ears

Tinnitus is the perception of sound that does not correspond to any external source. The most commonly perceived sound is ringing, but there are also whistles and pops, clicking and roaring. The disease is not well understood, although it affects hundreds of millions of people worldwide. The most common causes seem to be:

Damage to the cochlea: Sudden or continuous exposure to loud noise can damage this region of the inner ear. Ninety percent of cases have this cause.

Allergies: Probably linked to the buildup of pressure in the sinuses.

Stress: People with tinnitus often report that stress is a contributing factor in the onset of the condition.

Ménière's disease: A disorder of the inner ear that is not very well understood and that also causes vertigo.

"Bathykolpian" means big-breasted, from the Greek "bathus" (deep) and "kolpos" (cleft).

NICE FIGUR(INE)

The oldest-known representation of the human figure is the Venus of Hohle Fels, a 35,000-year-old figurine made of mammoth tusk, discovered in Germany in 2008. It was probably an amulet that symbolized fertility.

THIS SUCKS

For decades, the medical profession has been aware that open wounds heal more quickly under suction. If negative pressure is applied underneath a tightly sealed bandage, healing takes place more rapidly—no one knows why, but it could be that the lower pressure draws bacteria away from the wound and increases blood supply. Suction units are routinely used in disaster situations, but they are expensive, bulky, and need power. In 2010, students at the Massachusetts Institute of Technology developed a simple version that is cheap, lightweight, and needs no power.

Hand-powered suction unit developed at MIT.

Does my gluteus maximus look big in these?

Big and small

The largest muscle in the human body is the gluteus maximus (there are two, in the buttocks); the smallest, at just ⅕ inch (5 mm) long, is the stapedius (there are two of them, too, in the middle ears).

WHAT IS THIS?

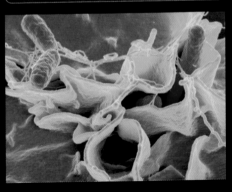

Answers on page 186.

Burning mystery

For more than 300 years, there have been reports of people spontaneously catching fire—with no apparent source of heat. In most cases, the body is almost completely destroyed, including the bones; normally, just the legs were left unburnt. The mystery of how bodies could burn so much was at least partly solved by experiments in 1998 using pig fat wrapped in clothing that was ignited by a blowtorch. The experiments showed how a body can behave like a candle, with the fat as the wax and clothing as a wick, allowing the body to burn slowly for hours and be almost completely consumed.

OUTER LAYERS

Cortex is a Latin word for a tree's bark. In anatomy, it is used to describe the outermost part of an organ. The cerebral cortex is the best-known example; it gives the brain its wrinkled, walnutlike appearance. Unfolded, the cerebral cortex would be about the size of a dish towel.

- **Ovarian cortex** (ovaries)
- **Renal cortex** (kidneys)
- **Adrenal cortex** (adrenal glands)
- **Thymic cortex** (thymus)
- **Cortex lentis** (lens of the eye)
- **Cerebellar cortex** (cerebellum)
- **Cerebral cortex** (cerebrum—the main part of the brain)

Cerebral cortex of the brain

A ROUGH GUIDE TO PUTTING ON WEIGHT 3,500 calories (kilocalories) is equivalent to one pound (0.45 kg) of body weight. If you consume 23,500 calories in a week but you use up only 20,000, you will be one pound heavier.

A world inside your gut

Your large intestine is teeming with microscopic life known as gut flora, which add up to about 16 trillion organisms per cubic inch (about 100 billion organisms per cubic cm) of its contents. Some of the microorganisms are beneficial—they break down indigestible parts of your food and provide up to 20 percent of your calorie intake, preventing allergies and manufacturing vitamin K. But some are not so good, increasing the risk of infection and even cancer. You can encourage the good ones to proliferate by eating "probiotics"—foods high in soluble fiber, on which the good bacteria thrive—such as soy beans, chicory root, and raw oats. Methane-producing organisms (methanogens), which account for methane in human flatulance, are present in only about 50 percent of the population.

Common species of gut flora:

♥ *Bacteroides melaninogenicus*

♥ *Bacteroides fragilis*

♥ *Bacteroides oralis*

♥ *Lactobacillus*

♥ *Enterococcus faecalis*

♥ *Bifidobacterium bifidum*

♥ *Staphylococcus aureus*

♥ *Escherichia coli (E. coli)*

♥ *Klebsiella oxytoca*

♥ *Klebsiella pneumoniae*

♥ *Enterobacter aerogenes*

♥ *Enterobacter cloacae*

♥ *Methanobrevibacter smithii* (methanogen)

♥ *Methanosphaera stadtmanae* (methanogen)

E. coli bacteria are part of the normal content of the digestive systems of humans and other animals. Some strains also cause food poisoning.

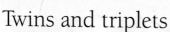

Since 2002, a clinic in the Netherlands has been offering eyeball jewelry—tiny decorative pieces of platinum alloy implanted directly into the conjunctiva.

NO CONTROL

Mature red blood cells are the only living cells in the human body that have no nucleus, the part that in other cells acts as the control center. Platelets, also in the blood, also have no nucleus—but they are fragments of cells, rather than cells proper. There are also cells in the outer layer of skin (the stratum corneum) that have no nucleus, but those cells are dead. The red blood cell starts off with a nucleus but loses it as it matures, to make more room in the cell for oxygen-carrying hemoglobin.

A red blood cell

Twins and triplets

In 1895, Polish pathologist Dyonizy Hellin (1867–1935) noted that the chance of a successful pregnancy giving rise to twins is about 1 in 89 (1.1 percent), while the chance of a successful pregnancy giving rise to triplets was 1 in 89^2 (1 in 7,921 or 0.013 percent). There is some variation across the world, but Hellin's Law still largely holds true. Since the advent of fertility treatments, in particular in vitro fertilization (IVF), the rate of multiple births has increased.

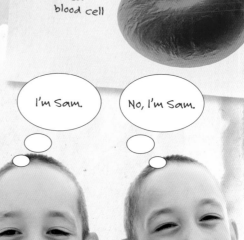

Identical twin boys

SOME WELL-KNOWN AUTOIMMUNE DISORDERS

... in which a body's immune system attacks its own tissues:

- ❦ Behçet's disease
- ❦ Type I diabetes
- ❦ Rheumatoid arthritis
- ❦ Celiac disease
- ❦ Crohn's disease
- ❦ Lupus (systemic lupus erythematosus)
- ❦ Multiple sclerosis (MS)

That full-up feeling

A hormone called ghrelin makes you feel hungry, so that you eat more, by affecting a part of the brain that controls appetite. It also affects the visual parts of the brain, making food look more attractive. Specialized cells in the stomach lining act as stretch receptors; when the stomach is empty, and those cells are relaxed, they produce lots of ghrelin, which makes you feel hungry. When the cells are stretched as the stomach becomes full, they produce less ghrelin, making you feel satisfied. Eating high-volume, low-calorie foods that pass out of your stomach slowly, such as vegetable soup, can satisfy your appetite for hours—a helpful tip for dieters.

Print of the first X-ray image, showing the ringed left hand of Anna Roentgen, 1895.

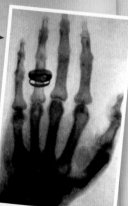

Print of an X-ray, taken by Roentgen in 1896, of the left hand of a colleague.

A penetrating gaze

In December 1895, the German physicist Wilhelm Conrad Roentgen became the first person to take an X-ray photograph through part of a human body. The photograph showed the bones in the hand of Anna, Roentgen's wife. One of the pioneers of X-ray medicine was British radiographer Major John Hall Edwards. His research into the dangers of over-exposure to X-rays involved his own body and resulted in the amputation of his own right hand. Later, the fingers of his left hand had to be amputated, too—and they can still be found in a jar in Birmingham, U.K.

HOW YOUR BRAIN SEES YOU

This image, called the sensory homunculus, represents a human body in which each part of the body is sized in proportion to the concentration of nerve endings in the skin in that region. The most sensitive areas, such as the fingertips and the lips, are much larger than other parts.

Don't laugh, I'm a sensitive person.

The stomach—the inside story

On June 6, 1822, American doctor William Beaumont tended to one Alexis St. Martin, a fur trader who had been shot accidentally with a musket. The shot took out some of St. Martin's lung and left a hole in his stomach. Incredibly, St. Martin survived the incident, and his wound healed over, apart from a small finger-sized opening that led directly into St. Martin's stomach.

Between 1825 and 1833, Beaumont carried out extensive experiments on St. Martin, including extracting digestive juices and inserting pieces of food into his stomach on a string, withdrawing them later to observe how the stomach processes food. Beaumont discovered that the digestive juices are more important in breaking food down than the stomach's muscular contractions.

Bone cells (osteoblasts), fat cells (adipocytes), and cartilage cells (chondrocytes) all develop from a single type of cell: the mesenchymal stem cell. This potential of a cell to develop into several different types is called "pluripotency."

Osteoblasts

Adipocytes

Mesenchymal stem cells

Chondrocytes

THE BODY'S ORGAN SYSTEMS

- 🍃 Cardiovascular system
- 🍃 Digestive system
- 🍃 Respiratory system
- 🍃 Nervous system
- 🍃 Reproductive system
- 🍃 Lymphatic system
- 🍃 Immune system
- 🍃 Endocrine system
- 🍃 Integumentary system
- 🍃 Musculoskeletal system
- 🍃 Urinary system

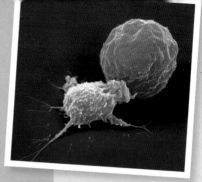

Cancer cell under attack from a natural killer cell.

Natural born killers

There is a killer in your midst—it's in your body: "natural killer" cells are one of the most important parts of your immune system. They kill cancerous cells and any cells that have been infected by viruses, by releasing special proteins that create holes in the cell membrane, followed by other proteins that destroy the cell or cause it to self-destruct.

It's hard work burning all these calories.

At rest, the average adult human body consumes energy at the rate of about 100 watts—equivalent to about one calorie (kilocalorie) every 40 seconds.

SWEET SENSATION

Lugduname, developed in the 1990s, is the sweetest compound known—it's about 250,000 times as sweet as sucrose (table sugar). In other words, a solution of lugduname can be one two-hundred-and-fifty-thousandth as strong as a solution of sucrose yet produce the same sweet sensation. The compound was developed during testing of a theory of sweetness known as the multipoint attachment theory, developed at the University of Lyon, France. The Latin name for Lyon is *Lugdunum*.

Table sugar

The total length of neuron fibers in the brain is an estimated 90,000 miles (150,000 km).

Right now I wish I was a chimpanzee.

Getting emotional

Most people who have studied crying agree that humans are the only animals who cry tears of emotion. While many other land animals have tear ducts that produce tears to keep their eyes moist and dust-free, not even our close relatives the primates—such as chimpanzees, lemurs, and monkeys—shed tears when they feel sad or scared. That's not to say that other animals don't feel these emotions—they just don't express them through crying.

Staring death in the face

Morgue is a French word meaning "haughtiness" or "contempt." In the 14th century, jailers at the Grand Châtelet building in Paris would stare at new inmates to intimidate them. Sometimes, corpses were taken to the same morgue rooms in the dungeons, for identification. Rooms set aside for that purpose gradually became known as morgues, and Americans adopted the term in the 19th century.

During that century, the main morgue in Paris became a popular tourist attraction. Every day, crowds of curious people stood one side of a glass partition, eager to see the naked corpses on the other side. Up to 12 bodies were on show at any time, kept fresh by running water. In November 1876, more than 130,000 people flocked to the morgue over a three-day period, when the dismembered body of a woman fished out of the River Seine went "on show."

Today, morgues are still used for a similar purpose—for storing corpses awaiting identification or post mortem examinations—albeit without the same public spectacle. In British English, the term "mortuary" is more commonly used—that word derives from the Latin word *mortuarium*, meaning "a place for the dead."

The entire central nervous system—the brain and spinal cord—is bathed in a clear liquid called cerebrospinal fluid. The total volume of this fluid is around 4.5 fluid ounces (130 ml). It is constantly replenished: the body makes around 17 fluid ounces (500 ml) every day.

Couldn't you make her a little more comfortable?

Bereaved visitors viewing corpses at a New York morgue, late 19th century.

An adult male head louse grips on to some human hair.

How to deal with nits

A nit is the egg of the human head louse (*Pediculus humanus capitis*). The word "nit" is sometimes also used for the newly hatched nymph. Head lice are parasites that survive by drinking blood. A louse bites into the scalp, using its saliva to prevent the blood clotting. When they are not drinking blood, head lice cling onto hairs and move from hair to hair using their claws—and they spend a lot of time mating. Female head lice lay eggs, which they attach to hairs using a very strong adhesive. The eggs hatch within a week, and after another week the nymphs are mature.

There are many different treatments for getting rid of a head louse infestation. Most treatments will kill or remove only adults, so a treatment should be repeated a few days later, to deal with the newly hatched nymphs.

How do I catch them?

☛ Head lice can't jump or fly, so you catch them through close contact.

☛ In some cases, you can get them from a towel or pillow (but they do not survive for long away from the head).

What are the symptoms?

☛ Sometimes there are no symptoms.

☛ Itchy scalp: particularly behind the ears and the back of the neck.

☛ Empty egg cases: these are white and are stuck firmly to your hair about an inch (2.5 cm) from your scalp.

Sugar high?

Contrary to popular belief, there is no evidence that eating lots of sugar makes children (or adults) hyperactive. The human body has a very efficient mechanism for storing away extra sugar, as well as for keeping the concentration of free sugar (glucose) within strict limits. Even if the concentration of sugar glucose in the blood rises above normal, your brain consumes the glucose on a need-to-use basis. Your brain's performance will suffer if your blood sugar is very low, but it does not become "supercharged" if the level is high.

A head louse egg fixed to a human hair.

Treatments?

- **Hot air:** Devices that blow hot air into the hair to dry out the lice and the eggs.
- **Wet-combing:** A fine-toothed comb passed from the roots to the tips of wet hair will sweep away most adult lice.
- **Wet-combing with hair conditioner:** You can loosen the lice's grip by using hair conditioner.
- **Pediculicide** (head louse insecticide): These don't always work and may cause scalp irritation.
- **Noninsecticide creams:** These coat lice, preventing them from breathing.

Always remember to follow up a few days later … and again a few days after that.

EMPTY VESSEL
The word "artery" comes from the Latin and Greek word "arteria," which means "air holder." Ancient anatomists believed arteries were air ducts because they do not contain any blood after death.

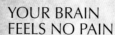

Look, it's like a giant mustache that goes all the way round my head!

YOUR BRAIN FEELS NO PAIN

Although the brain is where you "feel" everything, you would not feel pain if your brain itself was cut or bruised. As is the case with most other internal organs, the brain itself contains no pain sensors.

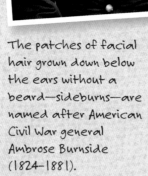

The patches of facial hair grown down below the ears without a beard—sideburns—are named after American Civil War general Ambrose Burnside (1824–1881).

High-impact colors

The amazing range of colors in some bruises is a direct result of the breakdown of hemoglobin, the oxygen-carrying molecule in red blood cells. Hemoglobin is red or purple (depending upon whether it is carrying oxygen). It breaks down to form biliverdin, which is greenish; biliverdin breaks down to form bilirubin, which is yellow; and bilirubin breaks down to form hemosiderin, which is brownish.

YOUR BODY NEEDS ...

... calcium

Nearly all the body's calcium—about 99 percent—is stored in the bones and teeth and is essential in making them strong. The remaining 1 percent is vital for muscle contraction, the dilation of blood vessels, the secretion of hormones, and the release of some neurotransmitters that allow neuron-to-neuron communication. Teenagers and pregnant women need higher daily amounts of calcium than other people. Foods high in calcium include dairy products such as milk, butter, cheese, and yogurt, green vegetables such as spinach, broccoli, and beans, and soft-boned fish such as salmon and sardines.

A calcium-rich salmon

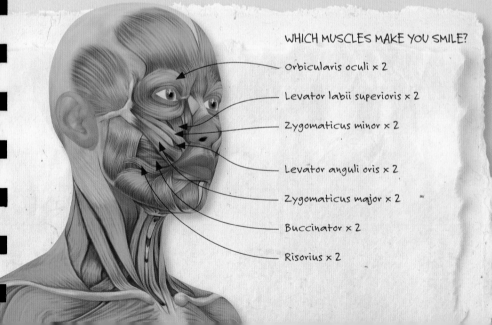

WHICH MUSCLES MAKE YOU SMILE?

— Orbicularis oculi x 2

— Levator labii superioris x 2

— Zygomaticus minor x 2

— Levator anguli oris x 2

— Zygomaticus major x 2

— Buccinator x 2

— Risorius x 2

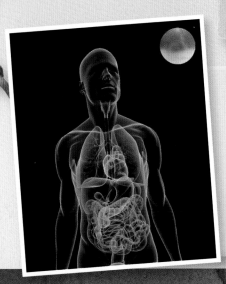

WHAT IS YOUR SPLEEN?

The spleen is about the size of a fist and is an important part of your lymphatic system, which helps fight infection and drains the body of excess fluid. It is particularly good at filtering out bacteria and any debris in the blood. It also removes dead red blood cells and salvages their iron content. You can live without your spleen—your liver will take over some of its function—but you will be much less able to fight infections.

Hair are you from?

Did you know that the water you drink can leave a "signature" in your hair that can be used to tell where you have been living. Water (H_2O) supplies vary in the ratio of isotopes—different versions of the same chemical element—of hydrogen (H) and oxygen (O). Some of the hydrogen and oxygen molecules find their way into molecules of keratin, the main protein in hair. In 2008, scientists from the University of Utah took nearly 500 samples of tap water from across the U.S.A. in order to map the different isotope ratios. Samples of hair from 65 barber shops in different towns had isotope ratios that matched the local water supply. The technique has been used to help police identify murder victims.

In medieval England, barbers cut the umbilical cord at a birth. Legend has it that the stripes on a barber's pole represent veins and arteries on the cord.

Keep that spacesuit on!

It is clearly not a good idea to venture into space without some kind of protection. A sudden "decompression" from normal atmospheric pressure inside a spaceship to the near vacuum of space would kill you quickly—but not as immediately or spectacularly as sometimes depicted in science fiction. The lack of outside air pressure would cause gases in your blood to come out of solution and water in your tissues to start boiling away—both of these processes would make your skin swell up. Your eardrums would probably burst and saliva would start boiling off your tongue. And it would be very cold out there in space. But none of these things would affect you straightaway, and these are not the things that would kill you.

Your blood is under pressure, and the first effects of exposure to a vacuum would be explosive hemorrhaging in the organ in which your blood comes closest to the outside world: inside your lungs. Within the first minute, the lungs would become badly ruptured and begin filling with blood. Your blood would not get any oxygen, and within about 15 seconds, your brain would start receiving deoxygenated blood—you would pass out around this time.

Despite all these traumatic and dramatic events, there is plenty of evidence from experiments on dogs and chimpanzees, and from a few accidents, that you would survive after as long as two minutes under extremely low pressures, with few long-term ill effects.

American astronaut Alan Shepard, who needed to keep his spacesuit on as he became the fifth person to walk on the Moon.

WHAT IS THIS?

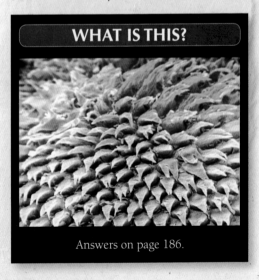

Answers on page 186.

The dark areas around the upper back in this PET scan of a woman indicate regions of brown fat.

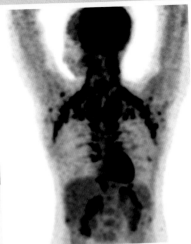

The word "penis" was originally a Latin word meaning "tail." "Penes" is an alternative medical plural to "penises."

Fat to make you slim?

Your body has two types of fat, or adipose tissue. The familiar white adipose tissue consists of cells each dominated by a single blob of fat. It is found under the skin and around internal organs and, in overweight people, in abundance in the belly, thighs, and around the buttocks. The second type is brown adipose tissue. Its cells contain less fat than their white counterparts, and the fat is dispersed among several tiny globules. Brown fat cells are also packed with more than their fair share of mitochondria—tiny powerhouses that convert food energy into a usable form inside the cells. The mitochondria give brown fat its color, and their presence in large numbers allows this strange tissue to generate heat.

Brown fat makes up 5 percent of an infant's body mass; it becomes active when the infant becomes cold, generating heat as a survival mechanism. Until recently, it was thought that brown fat disappears in adolescence, becoming white fat. But recent studies have shown that it is still present in adults; if scientists can find a way to activate brown fat, this knowledge could help people lose weight—and keep warm—by burning off excess calories.

YOU'LL (NOT) RUIN YOUR EYES!

Children are often told not to sit too close to a television screen, and not to read in dim light, for fear of "ruining their eyes." Focusing on nearby objects can cause fatigue of the eyes, known as eye strain (although children are better than adults at focusing on nearby objects without straining their eyes). In dim light, the eye's muscles have to work harder when changing focus between near and distant objects and may tire more quickly. But there is no evidence that eye strain "ruins" eyes.

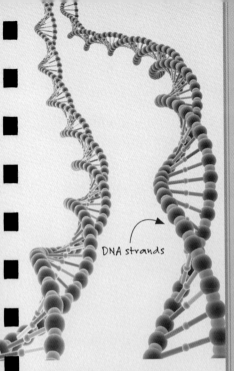

DNA strands

Tightly packed information

Each body cell—too small to see without a microscope—contains about 6 feet (2 m) of DNA (deoxyribonucleic acid). The DNA is wound around protein globules called histones, and these globules pack tightly together to form fibers. With an estimated 50 trillion (5×10^{13}) cells altogether, an adult human body contains a total of about 60,000 million miles (100,000 million km) of DNA. Stretched out and lined up end to end, all of the DNA molecules in a single human adult would stretch from Earth to the Sun and back nearly 70 times.

TLAs—THREE-LETTER ACRONYMS

❦ **ABC** Airway, Breathing, Circulation

❦ **ADP** Adenosine diphosphate

❦ **ALS** Amyotrophic lateral sclerosis

❦ **ATP** Adenosine triphosphate

❦ **CAT** Computed axial tomography

❦ **CJD** Creutzfeldt-Jakob disease

❦ **CNS** Central nervous system

❦ **CPR** Cardiopulmonary resuscitation

❦ **CSF** Cerebrospinal fluid

❦ **CVD** Cardiovascular disease

❦ **DNA** Deoxyribonucleic acid

❦ **ECG** Electrocardiography

❦ **EEG** Electroencephalography

❦ **EMG** Electromyography

❦ **FSH** Follicle-stimulating hormone

❦ **GFR** Glomerular filtration rate

❦ **hCG** Human chorionic gonadotropin

❦ **hGH** Human growth hormone

❦ **HIV** Human immunodeficiency virus

❦ **IGF** Insulin-like growth factor

❦ **IgG** Immunoglobulin G

❦ **ITP** Idiopathic thrombocytopenic purpura

❦ **MMR** Measles, mumps, rubella

❦ **MND** Motor neuron disease

❦ **MRI** Magnetic resonance imaging

❦ **PGD** Preimplantation genetic diagnosis

❦ **RNA** Ribonucleic acid

❦ **RTI** Respiratory tract infection

❦ **STI** Sexually transmitted infection

❦ **TSH** Thyroid-stimulating hormone

❦ **VZV** Varicella zoster virus

The largest bone in the body is the femur, or thigh bone, which is about one-quarter of a person's height.

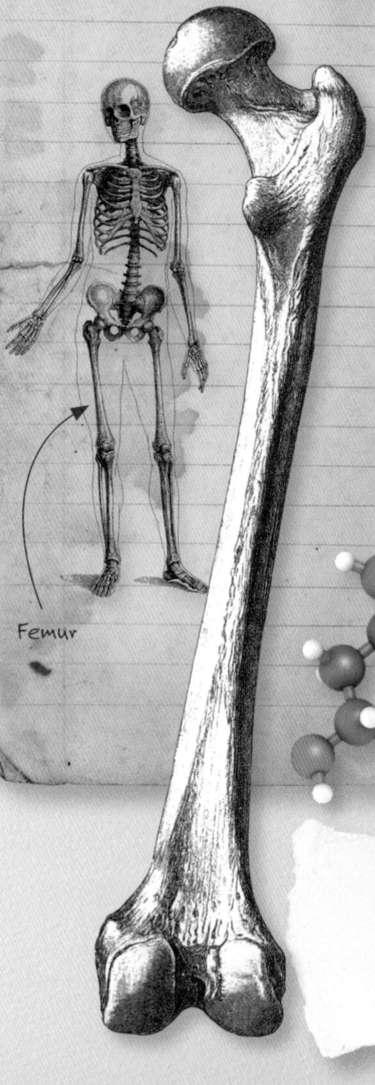

WHAT IS A STEROID?

If you must know, a steroid is any of hundreds of chemical compounds defined by a particular core molecular structure: three cyclohexane carbon rings and one cyclopentane ring! Here are the main categories, with some examples:

- **Sex steroids:** Hormones such as estrogen and testosterone.
- **Corticosteroids:** Hormones such as cortisol, produced in the adrenal glands (just above the kidneys).
- **Anabolic steroids:** Drugs that mimic the action of testosterone, typically increasing muscle mass.
- **Plant steroids:** Steroid hormones made by plants; foods rich in plant steroids can help to lower blood cholesterol.
- **Cholesterol:** A waxy substance carried in the blood inside globules called lipoproteins.

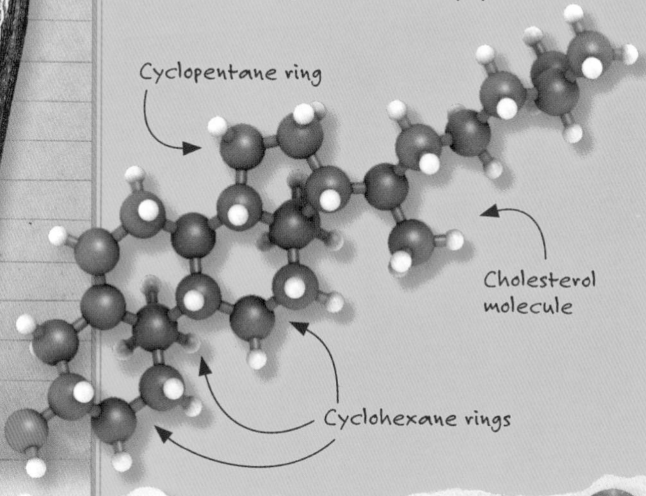

Bone up

Babies' skeletons are made of 350 "bones" that are actually made mostly of cartilage. As a baby grows, the bones harden, or "ossify," and some fuse together. An adult skeleton has only 206 bones.

Humans have the same pattern of bones in their limbs as all other vertebrates—the so-called pentadactyl limb has five fingers or toes. The lengths of its various bones vary from animal to animal.

Fox skeleton

Human skeleton

Bitter

Sour

Salty

Sour

Salty

Sweet

Bad taste

The popular map of the tongue—with distinct areas sensitive to sweet, sour, salty, and bitter tastes—is wrong, in two ways. First, every part of the tongue—and even the roof of the mouth—includes taste buds sensitive to all tastes. Secondly, there is a fifth basic taste type, with taste buds to match: it is called umami, or savory. The erroneous map arose in Germany at the beginning of the 20th century and was found to be mistaken only in the 1970s.

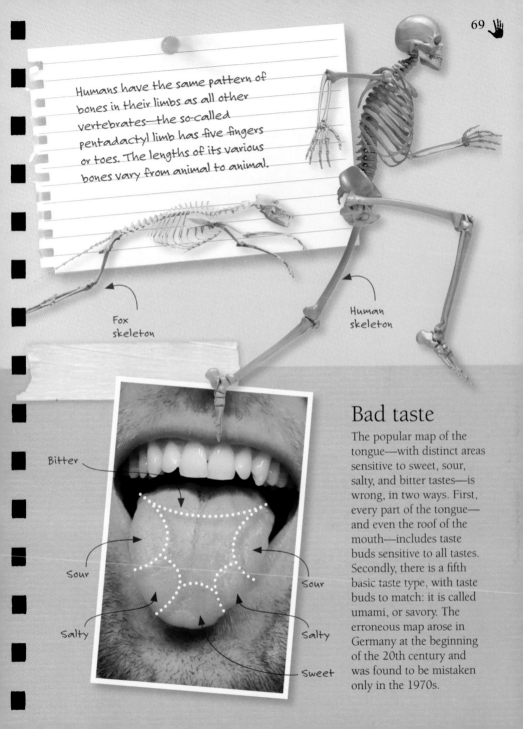

Humors—the best medicine?

Around 400 BCE, the ancient Greeks originated a theory that the body is composed of four "humors," or fluids: blood, phlegm, black bile, and yellow bile. To them, the purpose of digestion was to break food down into the humors, which could then be incorporated into the body's tissues. Illness was thought to be caused by an imbalance of the humors. For example, epilepsy was thought to be caused by an excess of phlegm, which blocked the windpipe and caused convulsions. Treatment was most often dietary, aiming to introduce the relevant humor into the body to address the balance. But bloodletting was also very popular, since blood was seen as the most dominant humor. The theory of the four humors persisted through the Roman Empire, among the Islamic scholars of the Middle Ages, and across Europe until the advent of modern medicine in the 19th century.

Asclepius, Greek
god of healing

ROOTS OF RESEARCH

In a number of controlled experiments, scientists have found that active compounds in ginger root—gingerol, zingerone, and shogaol—can have some amazing effects on the human body:

Ginger
root

♥ **Analgesic:** Kills pain

♥ **Anti-inflammatory:** Reduces damaging inflammation.

♥ **Antibacterial:** Helps fight infections.

♥ **Antiemetic:** Prevents vomiting, including sea sickness and morning sickness.

♥ **Anticancer:** Helps prevent bowel, pancreatic, ovarian, and breast cancers.

♥ **Antipyretic:** Reduces fever.

An average square inch of skin holds about 600 sweat glands, 25 blood vessels, and about 1,200 nerve endings.

That's me in the corner, dreaming

Sleep researchers have identified five distinct phases of sleep—N1, N2, N3, N4, and REM—each of which has a different pattern of brain activity. The phase in which we experience vivid dreams is REM (rapid eye movement) sleep. During this phase of sleep, our eyes flick backward and forward. No one really knows why we do this. The most obvious suggestion is that we are tracking objects moving in our dream, as we would do if they were real.

REM sleep was discovered and named in 1953 by American sleep researchers Nathaniel Kleitman and Eugene Aserinsky, although German physiologist Willhelm Graisinger had noted a connection between eye twitching and dreaming in 1868. REM sleep accounts for about one quarter of an adult's total sleep time but about three-quarters for a newborn baby. The brain's activity during REM sleep is similar to that when the brain is awake.

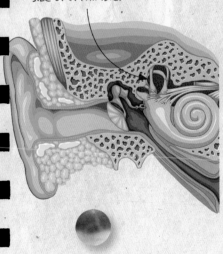

The vestibular system is about the size of a thimble.

TURNING HEADS

Your main organ of balance is the vestibular system, a set of three semicircular canals filled with a fluid called endolymph. When you move your head, the fluid moves, stimulating hairs on a membrane called the cupula, which sits at the junction of the canals. Each canal is at right angles to the other two, so your brain can work out if your head turned horizontally, vertically, from side-to-side, or some combination of these motions. The brain automatically makes the eyes compensate for the movement of your head—a movement called the vestibulo-ocular reflex.

If a person has a blood alcohol concentration of more than 0.04 percent, the cupula takes in some of the alcohol, which makes it less dense. This causes it to float in the endolymph, which makes it sensitive to gravity, leading to the impression that the head is constantly spinning if it is tilted only slightly—in other words, the person is drunk.

TOWARD THE BRAIN

To reach your brain from the outside world, an object would have to pass through several layers:

☞ Skin

☞ Periosteum (bone membrane)

☞ Bone (skull)

☞ Three meninges: dura mater, arachnoid mater, pia mater

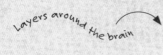

Layers around the brain

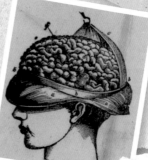

The word "avocado" is derived from the Central American word ahuacatl, meaning "testicle."

All in a day's work

The "basal metabolic rate" is the amount of energy your body uses each day just to keep you alive. It can be measured by a method called indirect calorimetry, which involves lying a person down for an hour under a hood and collecting the gases they exhale. The amount of energy their body is using can be calculated from the amount of oxygen they take in and the amount of carbon dioxide they breathe out. The BMR can be calculated by extrapolating the result to 24 hours. The measurement must be taken long enough after a meal so that no energy is being used in digestion; and the person should be resting, so that no energy is being used in physical exertion. The Harris-Benedict equation, created in 1919, provides a fairly accurate ready reckoning of your BMR in kilocalories (calories).

Imperial BMR formula

Women: BMR = 655 + (4.35 × weight in pounds) + (4.7 × height in inches) - (4.7 × age in years)

Men: BMR = 66 + (6.23 × weight in pounds) + (12.7 × height in inches) - (6.8 × age in years)

Metric BMR formula

Women: BMR = 655 + (9.6 × weight in kg) + (1.8 × height in cm) - (4.7 × age in years)

Men: BMR = 66 + (13.8 × weight in kg) + (5 × height in cm) - (6.8 × age in years)

YOUR BODY NEEDS ...

... sulfur

Your body contains about ½ ounce (15 g) of sulfur—there is a little in every cell. This nonmetallic element is essential in building proteins, including keratin, a major component of hair and skin. Sulfur also is important in building tendons, cartilage, and bone, and it plays a part in the liver's detoxifying process and in the digestion of fat.

Sulfur is a constituent of many protein molecules and so is readily available in most protein-rich foods. Particularly good dietary sources of sulfur include meat, eggs, garlic, onions, and green vegetables.

Good for your bones ... not so good for your breath!

Rock sulfur

It's like getting blood out of a skin.

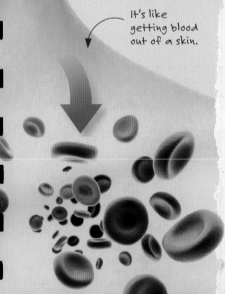

SKIN IS THICKER THAN WATER

In 2010, scientists at McMaster University in Ontario, Canada, succeeded at making blood from clumps of skin. The researchers managed to "reprogram" cells called fibroblasts, so that they would develop into blood cells. Fibroblasts are very common in skin and normally produce proteins such as collagen that hold skin together. The fibroblasts could be made to turn into oxygen-carrying red blood cells, infection-busting white blood cells, and blood-clotting platelets. The technique has the potential to generate blood for patients with leukemia and for cancer patients undergoing chemotherapy, which often knocks out the production of blood in a patient's bone marrow.

WHAT IS THIS?

Answers on page 186.

I'd better set my hypothalamus to defrost.

Your inner thermostat

The hypothalamus is a small part of the brain above the brainstem and just below the thalamus ("hypo" means "below"). One of its functions is to regulate core body temperature. It receives signals from nerve endings called thermoreceptors, which are present in various parts of the body.

If the core temperature falls below normal, the hypothalamus constricts arteries that supply blood vessels in the skin, to reduce heat loss. If the temperature falls very low, the hypothalamus sends messages to muscles that cause the body to shiver, which generates heat. If the temperature rises too high, the hypothalamus widens the blood vessels near the skin, to lose heat. The hypothalamus is also responsible for stimulating sweat glands to produce sweat when the body is hot; as the sweat evaporates, it cools the body.

The hypothalamus also sends messages to the pituitary gland, which sits next to it; the pituitary gland releases hormones that increase or decrease the metabolic rate—generating more or less heat.

Hypothalamus

Stealing a glimpse inside the body

At the age of just 16, Belgian student Andreas Vesalius stole a days-old corpse from the gallows. At the time, most anatomists did not work on human bodies—but Vesalius was hungry for knowledge. He went on to become a celebrated lecturer in anatomy and surgery at Padua, Italy, and in 1539 a judge there became interested in his work and made the bodies of criminals available to him. Vesalius used these bodies in his studies and his teaching. He used his lectures as the basis for a book: *De humani corporis fabrica* (On the Fabric of the Human Body), which was beautifully illustrated by artists from the school of Italian painter Titian. Vesalius' controversial book challenged many long-held beliefs that dated back to Roman anatomist Claudius Galen, who had carried out most of his studies on apes. It was the most influential anatomical book ever—and it was published in 1543, when Vesalius was just 28.

A drawing of muscles from Vesalius' book.

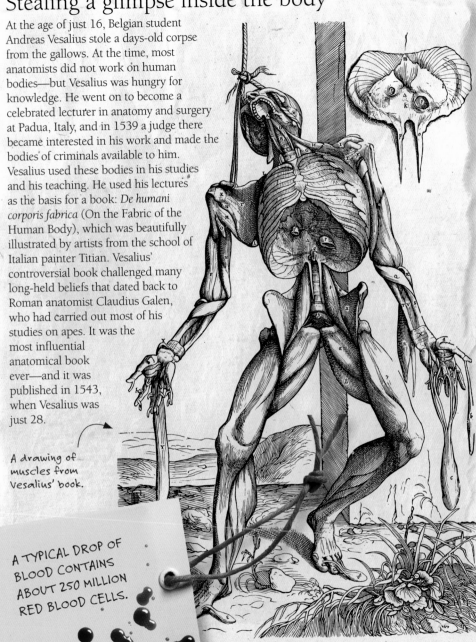

A TYPICAL DROP OF BLOOD CONTAINS ABOUT 250 MILLION RED BLOOD CELLS.

Free detox

Among its many other vital roles, the liver is your own personal detox organ. Using a family of about 60 enzymes called cytochrome P450, it breaks down potentially toxic compounds, including drugs such as caffeine. These enzymes also break down harmful products of chemical reactions in the body, such as bilirubin (from dead blood cells) and creatine. In a urine or blood test, the presence of substances normally broken down in the liver indicate there is a problem with liver function.

Location of the liver in the body

SMELL THE COFFEE AND WAKE UP

Caffeine keeps you awake because it blocks the action of your body's natural sleep-inducing chemical, adenosine. In the brain, adenosine inhibits the firing of neurons, slowing you down; it accumulates throughout the day, until you can take it no more, and you feel drawn to sleep. These two substances have molecular structures similar enough that caffeine fits snugly into receptors on cell membranes normally reserved for adenosine. As a result, caffeine blocks the action of adenosine, and this blocking action makes it an "adenosine antagonist." With no inhibition of neuron firing, your brain produces epinephrine, the fight or flight hormone, which raises your blood pressure, makes your pupils dilate, and opens your airways. It also constricts your blood vessels, which raises your blood pressure.

Elizabeth Ann Buttle, from Wales, gave birth to her first child, Belinda, on May 19, 1956. Her second child, Joseph, was born more than 41 years later—on November 20, 1997.

THE INSIDE STORY

The prefix "endo-," from Greek, means "internal":

❦ **Endocardium:** The inside lining of the heart.

❦ **Endochondroma:** A benign tumor of cartilage found inside bones.

❦ **Endocrine:** Describes the system of glands that secrete hormones directly into the bloodstream.

❦ **Endodontics:** The dental speciality dealing with the inside of the tooth.

❦ **Endogenous:** Describes any substance that is generated inside the body.

❦ **Endolymph:** The fluid inside organs of the inner ear.

❦ **Endometrium:** The inside lining of the womb.

❦ **Endoparasite:** A parasite that lives on the inside of the body.

❦ **Endophthalmitis:** Inflammation of the internal layers of the eye.

❦ **Endorphin:** A painkiller made inside the body— from "endogenous morphine."

❦ **Endoscope:** A device for viewing inside the body.

❦ **Endostasis:** Bone formation within cartilage.

❦ **Endothelium:** The inside surface of a blood vessel.

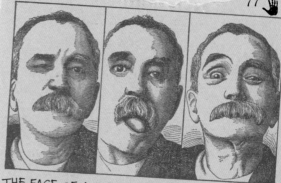

THE FACE OF ANXIETY

People with extreme emotional stress sometimes develop physiological symptoms such as paralysis or loss of sensation. These symptoms used to be called "hysteria" but are now referred to as "conversion disorder"—because anxiety is converted into physical symptoms.

Low fat

People with fat deposited low down on their bodies—whose hips are wider than their waist—are described as "pear-shaped." And scientists have found that fat in this location can actually promote health. Those whose fat is more concentrated around the waist are described as "apple-shaped." Fat inside the abdomen (visceral fat) constantly releases fatty acids (lipids) into the bloodstream, increasing the blood's "lipid profile." A high lipid profile increases the chance of developing cardiovascular disease, such as heart disease and stroke. Abdominal fat also releases hormones that increase the body's inflammation response, which can damage tissues, and also increases the risk of heart disease and diabetes. Hip and thigh fat, on the other hand, does not readily release fatty acids and produces a different hormone, called adiponectin, which seems to protect against cardiovascular disease.

Asclepius (center) with other Greek gods.

HEALING GOD

Asklepios, or Asclepius, was the Greek god of healing—his daughters were Hygienia ("Hygiene"), Iaso ("Medicine"), Akeso ("Healing"), Aglæa ("Grace"), and Panakeia ("Panacea" or "Universal Remedy").

Bumps on the head

Phrenology was the "science" of reading a person's character in the contours of their skull. It was devised by Austrian anatomist Franz Joseph Gall and was popular throughout the 19th century. The central idea of phrenology—that the shape of the skull depends on how well different functions are developed—has long been proven incorrect. The thickness of the skull varies, and the shape of its surface says nothing about the shape of the brain beneath. And even if it did, there is no way you can tell anything about a person's character from the shape of their brain.

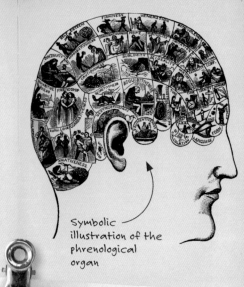

Symbolic illustration of the phrenological organ

SAY CHEESE

If you suffer from foot odor, it is not just because of the quarter of a million sweat glands on each foot—more per square inch than anywhere else on your body. The smell comes from bacteria that feed on the sweat—and they thrive all the better in the dark, enclosed conditions inside socks and shoes, where the sweat has little chance of escape. According to the U.S. Society of Chiropodists and Podiatrists, antibacterial soap is the best way to keep those bacteria at bay.

YOU'VE GOT A LOT OF GUTS

Any indigestible food leaving your stomach, such as insoluble fiber, has to travel a long way before leaving your body when you empty your bowels (digestible foods are absorbed into your body along the way and don't make the whole journey). The small intestine is about 20 feet (6 m) long, and the large intestine is about 5 feet (1.5 m) long—a total distance of around 25 feet (7.5 m). The time taken for the journey through those tubes depends upon how much liquid you drink and also how much fiber is in your food. A meal rich in fiber will pass through your system in as little as 24 hours; a low-fiber meal can take as long as 72 hours.

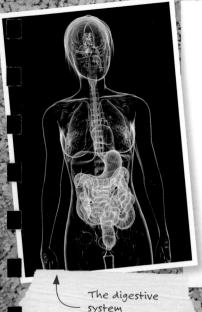

The digestive system

Placebo reward

A 2010 experiment by Canadian scientists gave tantalizing insight into the placebo effect—that weird phenomenon in which a fake medical intervention has real benefits. The experiment involved 35 patients with Parkinson's disease who were already receiving medication. In the experiment the patients were divided into four groups. One group was told that they had a 25 percent chance of receiving active medicine rather than a placebo, one group was told 50 percent, a third 75 percent, and another 100 percent—in other words, that they would definitely receive the active drug.

In fact, all the patients were given a placebo. The results were astounding: the group that was given a 75 percent chance of receiving the real drug released increased amounts of dopamine, low levels of which cause Parkinson's symptoms, but none of the other groups responded significantly. Dopamine is part of the brain's reward system: it controls behavior by inducing pleasurable effects. It seems that if an outcome is either certain or unlikely, there is no need to activate the reward system.

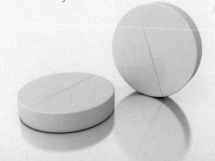

Sweet nothing

Despite its charming-sounding name, maple syrup urine disease is anything but charming. Babies born with this genetic disease appear healthy at first—the only symptom, and the reason for the name, is very sweet-smelling urine. But inside, there is a problem: the body fails to break down certain amino acids. Prompt treatment produces a recovery, but left untreated, this disease causes severe brain damage. It affects one in 180,000 people.

Maple syrup

The word "pugnacious," meaning "combative," derives from the Latin word "pugnus," meaning "fist."

YOUR BODY NEEDS ...

... iron

A healthy adult human body contains about 3–4 g of the element iron—about the same as in a small steel nail. More than half of the body's iron is locked up in molecules of hemoglobin in red blood cells. Meat contains "heme iron," while vegetables contain "non-heme" iron. Heme iron is more easily absorbed by the body than non-heme iron—and vitamin C helps to increase the absorption.

All meat and fish contains plenty of iron, while good vegetable sources include spinach, tofu, and raisins.

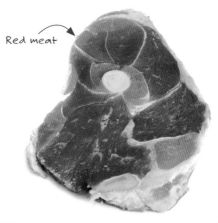

Red meat

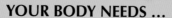

Steel nail

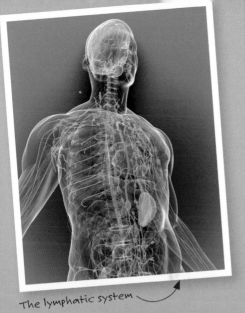

The lymphatic system

The vertical groove between your upper lip and the base of your nose is called the philtrum.

Soaking on the inside

An adult human body contains about 2.6 gallons (10 liters) of interstitial fluid, which fills the spaces between the cells of its tissues—"interstitial" literally means "between spaces." This fluid is produced by blood that leaks out through the walls of capillaries. Blood cells cannot pass through capillary walls, so interstitial fluid is just the liquid part—the plasma. It is mostly water, with nutrients, hormones, enzymes, and waste products dissolved in it. A small proportion of this fluid drains into the lymphatic system, which ultimately returns it to the blood.

Once in the lymphatic system the fluid—now called lymph—also carries bacteria and viruses from the body's tissues. Lymph nodes along the way contain white blood cells, which kill these invaders.

John George Haigh

CASE (DIS)SOLVED

In the 1940s, English murderer John George Haigh used a very unusual method to dispose of his victims: he dissolved their bodies in large drums of concentrated sulfuric acid and poured the resulting sludge down the drains. He was eventually captured when police found three gallstones and part of a denture from his last victim in sludge in his workshop.

Rheumatic fever has nothing to do with rheumatism. Rheumatic fever is the result of infection by streptococcal bacteria, whereas rheumatism is a term for a wide range of diseases that affect the joints—in particular, rheumatoid arthritis.

IT'S IN THE BLOOD

Anemia: Not enough iron in the blood.

Bacteremia: The presence of bacteria in the blood.

Hyperglycemia: Too much glucose (sugar) in the blood.

Hypoglycemia: Too little glucose in the blood.

Hypermagnesemia: Too much magnesium in the blood.

Hypernatremia: Too much sodium in the blood.

Leukemia: Cancer that results in too many white cells in the blood.

Polycythemia: Too many red blood cells in the blood.

Septicemia: Infection in the blood.

Toxemia: The presence of toxins in the blood.

Viremia: The presence of viruses in the blood.

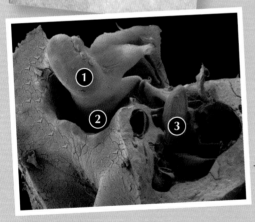

The malleus (1), incus (2), and stapes (3) bones of the middle ear are tiny: at ⅛ inch (3.3 mm), the stapes is the tiniest bone in the body.

Hammer, anvil, stirrup

The ossicles (tiny bones) in the middle ear are the smallest bones in the body. Their medical names—malleus, incus, and stapes—are Latin for hammer, anvil, and stirrup, and reflect their shapes. Together, they conduct vibrations of the eardrum through to the ear's sense organ, the cochlea.

The first cesarean section in which the woman is known to have survived took place around 1500, in Switzerland. It was carried out by a man who castrated pigs for a living.

Single-gene disorders

Some diseases are caused by a mutation in a single gene. Everyone has two copies of each of the 25,000 or so genes that make up the human genome. Some diseases will develop only if both copies of a particular gene are the "faulty" version. In such cases the disease is called "recessive"—and both parents must have at least one faulty copy of the gene. Some diseases develop when only one faulty version of the gene is present. These diseases are called "dominant"—a person need inherit only one copy of the faulty gene in order to develop the disease, so only one parent need have the faulty copy.

A further categorization depends upon whether the faulty gene occurs on the sex chromosomes (X or Y) or not—this can explain why some diseases affect only males, for example, but can be carried by females. The Y chromosome (carried only by males) is small, and most "sex-linked" single-gene disorders are "X-linked."

Chromosomes other than sex chromosomes are called autosomes, and disorders they cause are "autosomal." There are around 5,000 known single-gene disorders, and a baby is born with one of them once in every 200 or so births. Some of the most important or common are:

Cystic fibrosis: Autosomal recessive

Sickle cell anemia: Autosomal recessive

Huntingdon's disease: Autosomal dominant

Phenylketonuria: Autosomal recessive

Hemophilia (A and B): X-linked recessive

Duchenne muscular dystrophy: X-linked recessive

Polycystic kidney disease: Autosomal dominant

Familial hypercholesterolemia: Autosomal dominant

Tay-Sachs disease: Autosomal recessive

Neurofibromatosis, type 1: Autosomal dominant

About half of all breast cancer diagnoses in women are made in those between the ages of 50 and 70.

It's not funny—and it's not a bone

Everyone knows that the "funny bone" is not funny. But not everyone knows that it is not a bone at all: it is a nerve. When you hit your funny bone, you are actually whacking a nerve against a bone—and that creates a tingling sensation and can even be painful. The true identity of the funny bone is the ulnar nerve, which passes messages between your brain and part of your hand. It runs just beneath your skin and is particularly sensitive in the groove in the ulna bone, one of the two bones of the lower arm. The funny bone probably gets its name because the ulnar nerve runs along next to the bone called the humerus.

Ouch! That's not very humerus.

FRENCH PARADOX

In 1819, Irish doctor Samuel Black noticed that the rate of heart disease in France was surprisingly low, despite the relatively large amounts of saturated fats in the typical French diet. This "French Paradox" seems to still exist: according to the most recent statistics, deaths from heart disease in France amounted to 73 per 100,000 (2002) compared to 174 per 100,000 (2004) in the U.S.A. There are many possible reasons for the discrepancy, including the greater consumption of red wine in France; a compound present in red wine called resveratrol has been shown to reduce the risk of heart disease.

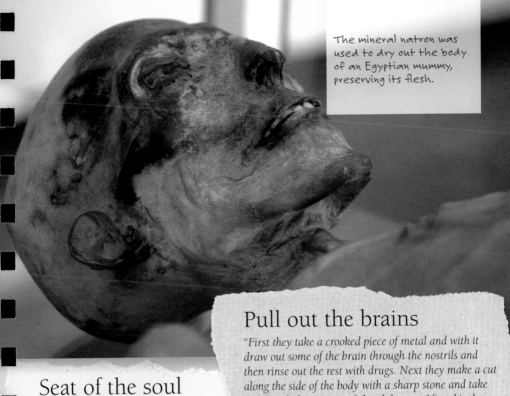

Pull out the brains

"First they take a crooked piece of metal and with it draw out some of the brain through the nostrils and then rinse out the rest with drugs. Next they make a cut along the side of the body with a sharp stone and take out the whole contents of the abdomen. After this they fill the cavity with myrrh, cassia and other spices and the body is placed in natron for 70 days."
Greek historian Herodotus, reporting on ancient Egyptian embalmers preparing a corpse for mummification in the 5th century BCE.

Seat of the soul

French philosopher, mathematician, and physicist René Descartes (1596–1650) was also an expert in anatomy. In the 1630s, he cut open an ox's eye and observed how the lens made an image on the retina. This left the problem of how the image is interpreted or "viewed." Descartes believed in the existence of a soul, which he believed was located in the pineal gland, located in the brain just behind the eyes. He wrote that the pineal gland was filled with "animal spirits" that were like "a very fine wind, or rather a very lively and pure flame."

Ox eye

The Museum of Zoology and Natural History in Florence, Italy, houses a collection of very realistic Wax anatomical models.

WAX WANED

During the 18th century, wax became the most popular material for making anatomical models. The first examples came from Italy, but the practice quickly spread across Europe. The models were normally produced by artists working with professors of anatomy, so they were prized for their detail and artistic qualities. But they were expensive and fragile and ultimately their popularity waned. In the 19th century a new material replaced wax: papier mâché. Today, models are mass-produced using plastics.

What's that smell?

Many people are aware of a strange phenomenon that occurs after eating asparagus: their urine has a pungent smell. The culprit is a sulfur-containing compound called methanethiol, which imparts an odor like rotten cabbage. Whether or not a person produces this compound in their urine after eating asparagus is determined by their genes—and it affects only about 40 percent of people.

Asparagus

BLOODY SAYINGS
- My blood runs cold
- Hot-blooded
- In cold blood
- Written in blood
- Bad blood
- Blood out of a stone
- New blood
- Sweating blood

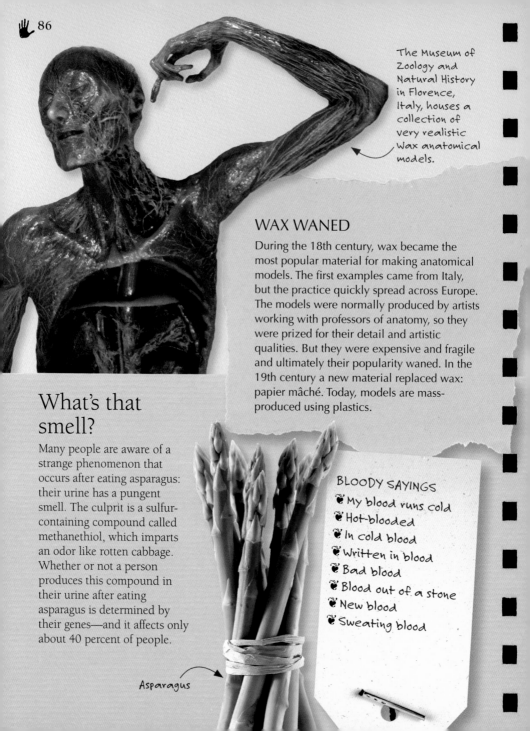

PROTEINS

There are tens of thousands of different proteins in the human body. Some protein molecules are "building blocks," making up hair and fingernails, most of your skin and bone—and filling every cell as an internal "cytoskeleton" that keeps the cell from collapsing in on itself. Some proteins play vital roles in the millions of reactions that keep you alive; a special and very important case is enzymes, which are proteins that help make other chemical reactions happen, but don't take part in the reaction themselves.

Collagen: Found in tendons, cartilage, bone, blood vessels, skin, and the cornea, collagen is the most abundant protein, accounting for about 27 percent of the total dry weight of the human body.

Myosin: Together with actin, myosin makes up filaments called myofibrils inside muscle fiber cells. The filaments are attached to each end of a cell and when they contract, the cells contract, causing the muscle to contract as a whole. Some myosin proteins carry out essential processes inside cells, including playing a part in cell division.

Actin: Together with myosin, actin makes myofibrils inside muscle fibers; it is also a major component of the cytoskeleton of all cells.

Keratin: The main protein in the outermost layer of skin; also the main structural component of hair and nails.

Osteocalcin: A major component of bones and teeth, osteocalcin is also carried in the blood, playing a role in controlling blood sugar level.

Albumin: The most abundant protein dissolved in blood plasma, where its main job is to carry essential compounds, including certain hormones and fats.

Globulins: Carried in blood plasma, some globulins are antibodies produced by the immune system; other globulins are transport proteins, for carrying compounds such as fats and minerals such as copper.

Hemoglobin: Red blood cells are packed with this protein, which carries oxygen.

Elastin: A protein in skin and blood vessels that gives elasticity; we produce less elastin as we age.

The word "hippocampus" is the Latin term for "seahorse."

Hippocampus

The part of the brain that acts like a computer disk's read-write head for long-term memory is the hippocampus. In fact, like most structures in the brain, there are two hippocampi. They are constantly fed data that relates to your sensory experience of the world, and they "write" that experience to long-term memory. When the time comes to recall a memory, it is the hippocampi that "read" it. The hippocampi sit in the lining of the two largest fluid-filled spaces in the brain and are "plugged into" the brain's frontal lobe, in which most of the brain's higher processes take place. Damage to the hippocampi affects a person's long-term memory—and it is this part of the brain that is one of the first to be damaged in Alzheimer's disease.

Fever in the morning, fever all through the night

There are many different medicines that can reduce fever—but medical opinion is divided as to whether it is a good idea. Fever is part of your body's natural response to infection, and it has several benefits that can help deal with invading bacteria or viruses. Most of these invaders are very sensitive to temperature, and fever can really make them feel the heat and slow their proliferation.

Raising the temperature also increases your body's production of white blood cells—your first line of defense—and improves their performance. In most infections a fever increases body temperature from its normal level of about 98.6°F (37.0°C) by only about 3°F (1–2°C). Whether you try to reduce a minor fever with medicines or not, you should definitely act if your temperature approaches 104°F (40°C). Anything above 106°F (41°C) indicates extreme fever, which can be very serious. In this case, medical attention should be sought immediately.

BRISTOL STOOL SCALE

Developed at the University of Bristol, U.K., in the 1990s, the Stool Scale is a useful standard for classifying stools—for medical records and research purposes. Generally, the harder a stool, the longer it has spent in the colon. Diarrhea (Type 7) has spent the least amount of time. Type 4 is generally considered the ideal stool in terms of health.

Type 1	Separate, hard lumps, like nuts (hard to pass)
Type 2	Sausage-shaped but lumpy
Type 3	Like a sausage but with cracks on its surface
Type 4	Like a sausage or snake, smooth and soft
Type 5	Soft blobs with clear-cut edges (passed easily)
Type 6	Fluffy pieces with ragged edges, a mushy stool
Type 7	Watery, no solid pieces, entirely liquid

Stay away from my brain

Your brain and spinal cord enjoy special privileges: they are isolated from the everyday chemical chaos of the rest of your body by a system that grants exclusive access only to certain molecules. Your "blood-brain barrier" protects your brain from potentially harmful substances in the blood—and it ensures that hormones and neurotransmitters meant for your body tissues do not get in and affect your brain. It also keeps bacteria and viruses out. But how does it work?

In most parts of the body, the cells lining your blood capillaries are not packed too closely together and there are tiny spaces between them. The spaces allow large molecules to pass through from the blood to the surrounding tissues. Bacteria and viruses can also pass through—but so can the white blood cells of your immune system that defend against these invaders. The cells lining the capillaries that supply the brain are different: they are tightly joined together,

so that they form an impermeable tube. Cell membranes are composed of oils, so water-soluble substances have no direct access through the barrier. Some small fat-soluble substances do pass through—including some vitamins—but also caffeine, alcohol, and nicotine. Fortunately, certain vital molecules are allowed through because of specialized transport mechanisms in the cell membranes; so, glucose and oxygen actually pass through the cells. Brain-side, there is another layer consisting of cells called astrocytes, which add further protection for the brain.

The blood-brain barrier is absent in the pituitary gland. It deteriorates with age and can be compromised under high blood pressure. And when pathogens do get through the barrier, they can cause real harm that is difficult to deal with, since the white blood cells and other products of your body's immune system cannot get through.

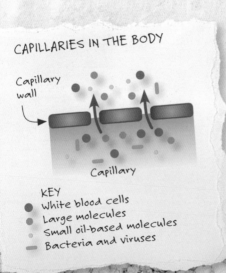

CAPILLARIES IN THE BODY

Capillary wall

Capillary

KEY
● White blood cells
● Large molecules
● Small oil-based molecules
— Bacteria and viruses

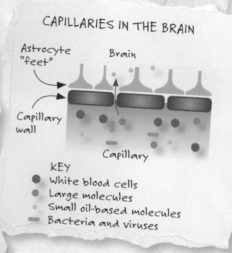

CAPILLARIES IN THE BRAIN

Astrocyte "feet"

Brain

Capillary wall

Capillary

KEY
● White blood cells
● Large molecules
● Small oil-based molecules
— Bacteria and viruses

Heavy, man

English jailer Daniel Lambert was famous for being fat. In 1805, aged 35, he weighed 50 stones, or 700 pounds (320 kg). At the time, he was the heaviest man known—but many people have dwarfed his record since then. The heaviest-known man who has ever lived so far was Jon Brower Minnoch, from Seattle, Washington. When he was 35, he weighed in at 69 stones 9 pounds, or 974 pounds (442 kg). His weight then began to soar, as his body began to retain huge amounts of fluid. At the time he was too large to be weighed properly, but his weight was an estimated 100 stones, or 1,400 pounds (635 kg). The heaviest-known woman who has ever lived was Carol Yager, from Beecher, Michigan, whose confirmed highest weight was 85 stones 10 pounds, or 1,200 pounds (545 kg).

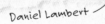

Daniel Lambert

Ninety percent of food allergies are caused by nuts and peanuts, milk, eggs, soy, wheat, fish, and shellfish.

Never judge a book by its cover

Leather-bound books are uncommon today, but they were once the norm. In the 17th and 18th centuries, it was not unusual for the leather to have been made from human skin, which typically came from unclaimed bodies. The practice of binding a book in human skin is called anthropodermic bibliopegy.

FEEL THE BEAT OF YOUR HEART

It is easiest to detect a pulse in arteries that lie close to the skin and can be pressed against bone. To calculate beats per minute (bpm), count how many pulses there are in 15 seconds and multiply by four. The normal ranges are: adults, 60 to 100 bpm; children, 70 to 120 bpm; toddlers, 90 to 150 bpm.

Here are some of the best places to feel a pulse:

Facial artery: Press your fingers onto the neck down from the ears and just beneath the jaw bone; the facial artery is one of the branches from the carotid and is often easy to find.

Radial artery: Press your index and middle fingers firmly on the palm side of the person's wrist, on the thumb side. Come in about half an inch (1 cm) from the hard bone (the radius) on the thumb side of the wrist.

Brachial artery: This runs alongside the biceps, and it can be hard to find. Hold the arm extended, palm up, and follow an imaginary line from the little finger to the elbow crease. Hold two fingers flat there—not just the fingertips—and you should be able to feel it.

Popliteal artery: This artery runs through the hollow behind the knee. To find it, raise one leg on a chair, knee bent, place all your fingers behind the knee, and press into the soft area (the popliteal fossa).

Femoral artery: Think of an imaginary line running from the hip to the groin. Press two fingers in at a point two-thirds along the line, starting from the hip.

Dorsalis pedis artery: Hold two fingers on top of the foot, on the inner side, along an imaginary line that joins the big toe to the ankle.

Superficial temporal artery: Press two fingertips onto the temple, halfway between the outside edge of the eye and the top of the ear.

Checking the pulse on the radial artery

The speed of a sneeze is about 35–40 mph (55–66 kph), not the often-quoted figure of 100 mph (160 kph), according to measurements in the television series "Mythbusters."

Inner fire

Your body's main fuel is glucose, a simple sugar that is produced by breaking down carbohydrates contained in food (or directly available in some snacks and sports drinks). When your blood glucose rises above a certain level, your pancreas releases insulin into the blood. The insulin causes glucose to be stored in the liver and muscles in a concentrated form called glycogen. The glycogen is converted back into glucose if the concentration of blood glucose falls below a certain level.

About one-tenth of the mass of your liver is glycogen, but only about one-hundredth the mass of a muscle. The average person typically holds about 14 ounces (400 g) of glycogen in total, equivalent to about 1,500 calories.

Some glucose is also converted into fat, which provides a much more concentrated method of storing energy—it's about six times more energy-dense than glycogen but is less readily available. If you are doing demanding exercise, most of the energy will come from the readily available glycogen.

Many long-distance athletes are familiar with hitting "the wall," which corresponds to the depletion of your glycogen supplies, so that your body has to switch to the harder-to-get-at fat for its energy needs. This results in a rapid decline in performance and is why "carbohydrate loading" helps athletes avoid hitting the wall.

Energy
from glucose
in blood

Energy
from
glycogen

The wall

Energy
from fat

Boy or girl?

Until about the ninth week of gestation, male and female fetuses are physically indistinguishable. The production of different hormones in male and female fetuses brings on changes that make various structures develop in different ways, or disappear altogether, leading to the development of male and female reproductive organs. So, for example, the fallopian tubes and the uterus develop from structures called Müllerian ducts; a male fetus produces a hormone called Müllerian duct inhibitor, which causes these ducts to atrophy (waste away). Another hormone, called human chorionic gonadotropin, causes a male fetus to produce testosterone, which in turn causes structures called Wolffian ducts to develop into the tubes that carry sperm. In female fetuses, the Wolffian ducts atrophy.

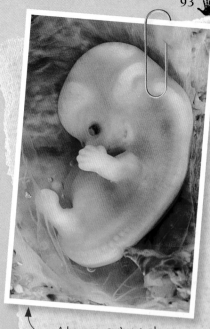

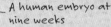
A human embryo at nine weeks

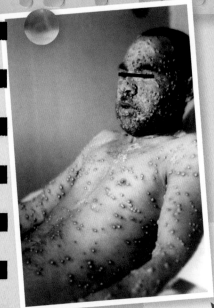

ALL GONE?

Smallpox was the first human disease in history to be completely eradicated. There were many smallpox epidemics through recorded history, which caused hundreds of millions of deaths. Thanks to widespread vaccination, the disease declined in the 19th and 20th centuries; the last natural case was diagnosed in 1977, and on May 8, 1980, the World Health Assembly declared the world free of smallpox. There are a few small samples of the virus in two laboratories, one in the U.S.A. and one in Russia.

The smallpox lesions on this Iranian man would have formed scabs that would fall off leaving marks on the skin. The patient is contagious until all of the scabs are gone.

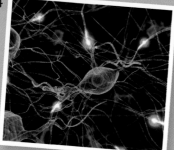

How many neurons?

The total number of neurons in the human brain is often given as around 100 billion (1 followed by eleven zeros). This has traditionally been estimated by taking thin sections of brain and counting cells under a microscope—and then scaling up that count to a whole brain. The problem with this method is that the density of neurons is not constant, so any particular brain region may not be representative of the brain overall.

In 2005, scientists in Brazil developed a quicker and more accurate method for counting brain cells. Their method, dubbed "isotropic fractionation," involves breaking down the cell membranes and mixing the resulting mush into a liquid. In this solution, the nuclei are evenly spaced, and the scientists can count the number of nuclei in a given volume of liquid and scale up their count more confidently. The technique was applied to the human brain in 2009. It turns out that your experience of the world, your memory, your behavior, and the control over your body are accomplished by a total of around 85 billion neurons.

WHAT IS THIS?

Answers on page 186.

Uncontrolled closing of the eyelids is called blepharospasm. It can be caused by stress, fatigue, or disease—or by irritation by chemicals, including the active compound of spicy foods, capsaicin.

I wish I knew what this blinking problem is called.

COMMON CHILDHOOD RASHES, THEIR SCIENTIFIC NAMES AND THEIR CAUSES

Rash	Scientific name	Cause
Measles	Rubeola	Morbillivirus
Roseola infantum	Exanthema subitum	Human herpes virus 6 and 7
German measles	Rubella	Rubella virus
Scarlet fever	Scarletina	Streptococcus pyogenes
Fifth disease	Erythema infectiosum	Parvovirus B19

YOUR BODY NEEDS ...

... zinc

A healthy adult human body contains about 2 or 3 g of the metallic element zinc. Zinc has many important roles in fundamental biological processes, such as cell division and building proteins and DNA. It is involved in healing wounds, and in the action of nerves—our senses of taste and smell particularly depend upon zinc. Semen contains a relatively high concentration of zinc. The food with the most zinc per serving is oysters. Other good sources include crab, dairy products, nuts, and whole grains.

Oysters

DON'T PUSH IT!

Earwax—the proper name is cerumen—is a mixture of dead skin cells, an oily substance called sebum, and sweat. The sebum comes from sebaceous glands, which are also found all over the body wherever there are hair follicles. The purpose of earwax is to clean the ears and lubricate the skin in your ears; it traps dust particles and slowly transports them out, keeping them from reaching the eardrum. Earwax is also slightly acidic, and this makes for an inhospitable environment for bacteria.

Attempts to remove earwax using a cotton swab often push the mixture further down the ear canal. This may cause a blockage and is a common cause of hearing loss. There is normally no need to clean the wax, since it finds its own way out! But if an uncomfortable buildup does cause hearing loss, a few drops of baby oil in the ear can dissolve and loosen it. If that fails, a medical professional can remove earwax quickly and safely.

Exercise (and) your brain

Exercise can help your brain to stay more focused—improving your memory, reasoning power, creativity, and mood. Part of the reason for this is that physical exercise increases the brain's production of a protein called brain-derived neurotrophic factor. This protein helps developing neurons to survive and promotes the growth of new ones.

Code of life

The DNA in the chromosomes inside a single human cell carries about 1.4 gigabytes of information. This amount of information, in binary form, could be used to convey about 250 copies of the complete works of Shakespeare or about 5 minutes of full high-definition video (with full surround sound, of course). Sperm and egg cells have only half the total amount each, and red blood cells have no chromosomes at all.

Don't stress it!

The hormone cortisol, also known as hydrocortisone, is well known as a "stress hormone": it is released by the adrenal glands, which sit on top of each kidney—the same glands that release epinephrine (adrenaline). While epinephrine is a fast-acting "fight or flight" hormone that raises heart and breathing rates, cortisol is released after stressful events, to help restore the body to normal. Epinephrine causes a drain on the body's available energy, whereas cortisol raises it again and also mobilizes fats and even proteins as energy sources.

Cortisol also reduces the body's response to injury or infection (inflammation)—this is why there are many "hydrocortisone" creams, which are used to treat rashes caused by the skin's response to allergy or insect bites. While cortisol is undoubtedly a vital hormone, if you suffer stress most of the time, then some of its effects can be harmful: it raises blood pressure; by reducing inflammation, it can increase the chance of illness; it lays down fat around the organs in the abdomen, which may lead to dangerous "central obesity" and increases the risk of type II diabetes; it increases appetite; and it reduces bone density. Although short-term raised levels of cortisol enhance memory and learning, there is evidence that prolonged raised levels can impair learning.

The least invasive cortisol test involves a sample of saliva—more accurate results can be gained by testing blood or urine. The concentration of cortisol in the blood varies with the time of day and from person to person, but at 9 a.m., most adults have about 0.0001 g per liter of blood—a total throughout the body of about 0.0006 g.

My adrenal gland is really stressing me out ...

The scientific term for some people's habit of grinding their teeth and clenching their jaw is "bruxism."

In a heartbeat

In the second half of the 19th century, a few people had become interested in the electrical activity of the heart—but none had devised a method of measuring and recording it nor realized its potential use as a diagnostic tool. In 1903, after three years of painstaking experimentation, Dutch physiologist Willem Einthoven invented the first practical electrocardiograph. He went on to show how various heart problems could be recognized from an electrocardiogram (ECG) trace.

- 0.00s

The familiar shape of an electrocardiogram reveals the electrical activity associated with the various stages of a heartbeat.

Snatiation is an inherited condition in which the affected person sneezes uncontrollably whenever their stomach is full.

AMINO HARM

Amino acids are generally good for you: your body needs them, to build proteins. But there is one that is not so good—it appears to cause real harm. Elevated levels of an amino acid called homocysteine are associated with cardiovascular disease, thrombosis (unwanted blood clots), kidney damage, and, in the elderly, brittle bones.

A thrombus (blood clot) protruding from an arterial entrance in a chamber of the heart

TAKING IN THE CYTES

The suffix "-cyte" means "cell"; it comes from the Greek *kytos*, meaning "hollow."

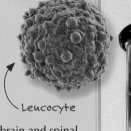

Leucocyte

Adipocytes: Fat-storing cells.

Astrocytes: Star-shaped cells in the brain and spinal cord that provide support to neurons.

Chondrocytes: Cells that produce cartilage.

Erythrocytes: Red blood cells.

Granulocytes: White blood cells that appear to have granules inside them. There are three types: neutrophils, eosinophils, and basophils.

Hepatocytes: The most common type of liver cell; have a vital role in the body's "chemical factory."

Keratinocytes: The most common type of cell in the outer layer of skin; they produce the protein keratin.

Leukocytes: The general name for white blood cells.

Lymphocytes: White blood cells that recognize particular invading organisms or substances: killer cells, T- and B-lymphocytes.

Megakaryocytes: Cells in the bone marrow that produce thrombocytes.

Melanocytes: Cells found at the bottom of the outermost layer of your skin; they produce the pigment melanin.

Monocytes: A type of phagocyte involved in targeted immunity.

Oligodendrocytes: Cells in the brain that help support neurons.

Oocytes: Immature egg cells.

Phagocytes: White blood cells that "eat" bacteria and other foreign substances.

Pneumocytes: Cells that help maintain the inner surfaces of the lungs.

Spermatocytes: Immature sperm cells.

Thrombocytes: Also known as platelets; cell fragments involved in clotting.

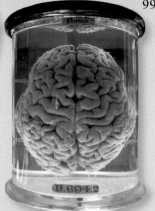

Making a meal of it

A living human brain—or one fresh out of the box—is pinkish and has the consistency of jello: almost as bouncy as a boiled egg, but not that firm; but as squelchy as soft tofu; as gelatinous as cold porridge; and as fatty as room-temperature butter; just think of your head as filled with thick custard.

If a brain needs to be studied in a postmortem or for scientific research, this sloppy organ must be treated, to make it firmer. First, the brain is soaked in a formaldehyde solution for three or four weeks—for this reason, some bodies are buried without their brains (but only with relatives' permission). After soaking, the brain is gray and has the consistency of canned mushrooms. It can now be sliced and examined under the microscope.

Don't sell your body

eBay has strict policies about selling human body parts. The exact policy varies from country to country, but in the U.S.A., it includes the following:

"We don't allow humans, the human body, or any human body parts or products to be listed on eBay, with two exceptions. Sellers can list items containing human scalp hair, and skulls and skeletons intended for medical use." Some items are excluded specifically: Native American grave-related items, Tibetan prayer skulls, organs, bones, blood, waste products, body fluids, sperm, eggs.

For Sale

Milk, anyone?

A tiny proportion of people are lactose intolerant at birth because of a rare genetic disorder, and babies with this disorder cannot digest their own mother's milk. The condition used to be fatal, until the invention of lactose-free formula milk. Everyone else produces plenty of an enzyme called lactase, which breaks down lactose, the main sugar found in milk.

Lactase production decreases with age, and some people stop producing it altogether. Some ethnic groups tend to develop a natural deficiency of lactase after childhood—in particular, those whose origins are in Asia, South America, and Africa, as well as Native Americans. Some people become lactose intolerant as the result of a disease, such as celiac disease. Nearly half of women who are lactose intolerant regain the ability to digest lactose during pregnancy.

As lactose passes through the digestive system of someone who is lactose

intolerant, it draws water into the small intestine, by osmosis. This ultimately makes the person's stools watery and speeds up the transit of food through the system, which means other food present may not be fully digested. In the large intestine, bacteria break down the lactose, producing hydrogen, methane, and acid as by-products. The hydrogen can be picked up in a breath test—the most common way of diagnosing the condition. As a result of the gas, lactose intolerance causes bloating and discomfort and flatulence whenever an affected person consumes milk products.

IMPROBABLE RESEARCH …

The Ig Nobel Committee awards annual prizes for research that "make people LAUGH and then THINK." There are prizes in several disciplines, including Medicine. Here are a few of the most entertaining (yes, they are all genuine):

1991 Alan Kligerman, deviser of digestive deliverance, vanquisher of vapor, and inventor of Beano, for his pioneering work with anti-gas liquids that prevent bloat, gassiness, discomfort, and embarassment.

1992 F. Kanda, E. Yagi, M. Fukuda, K. Nakajima, T. Ohta, and O. Nakata of the Shisedo Research Center in Yokohama, for their pioneering research study "Elucidation of Chemical Compounds Responsible for Foot Malodour," especially for their conclusion that people who think they have foot odor do, and those who don't, don't.

1993 James F. Nolan, Thomas J. Stillwell, and John P. Sands, Jr., medical men of mercy, for their painstaking research report, "Acute Management of the Zipper-Entrapped Penis."

1994 This prize was awarded in two parts. First, to Patient X, formerly of the U.S. Marine Corps, valiant victim of a venomous bite from his pet rattlesnake, for his determined use of electroshock therapy—at his own insistence, automobile sparkplug wires were attached to his lip, and the car engine revved to 3,000 rpm for five minutes. Second, to Dr. Richard C. Dart of the Rocky Mountain Poison Center and Dr. Richard A. Gustafson of The University of Arizona Health Sciences Center, for their well-grounded medical report: "Failure of Electric Shock Treatment for Rattlesnake Envenomation."

1995 Marcia E. Buebel, David S. Shannahoff-Khalsa, and Michael R. Boyle, for their invigorating study, "The Effects of Unilateral Forced Nostril Breathing on Cognition."

Continued on page 102

Egg

Egg cells, or ova, are the largest human cells. At slightly more than 1/200 inch (120 microns, or 0.12 mm), an ovum is just visible to the human eye. It is 16 times as big as a red blood cell—and slightly smaller than the point of a tack or this period. Eggs develop from precursor cells called oocytes—pronounced "o-o-sites," and normally one egg is released, from one of a woman's ovaries, each month of her reproductive life.

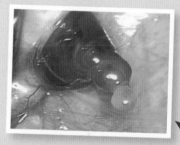

In 2008, gynecologist Professor Jacques Donnez, at the Catholic University of Louvain, Belgium, caught the moment of egg release—ovulation—magnified on camera during a hysterectomy operation.

Dutch people have the largest average adult height; the average height of men is 6 feet and ½ inch (1.84 m), and the average height of women is 5 feet 7 inches (1.7 m).

Continued from page 101

1996 James Johnston of R.J. Reynolds, Joseph Taddeo of U.S. Tobacco, Andrew Tisch of Lorillard, William Campbell of Philip Morris, Edward A. Horrigan of Liggett Group, Donald S. Johnston of American Tobacco Company, and the late Thomas E. Sandefur, Jr., chairman of Brown and Williamson Tobacco Co., for their unshakable discovery, as testified to the U.S. Congress, that nicotine is not addictive.

1997 Carl J. Charnetski and Francis X. Brennan, Jr. of Wilkes University, and James F. Harrison of Muzak Ltd. in Seattle, Washington, for their discovery that listening to elevator Muzak stimulates immunoblobulin A (IgA) production, and thus may help prevent the common cold.

1998 To Patient Y and his doctors, Caroline Mills, Meirion Llewelyn, David Kelly, and Peter Holt, of Royal Gwent Hospital, Wales, for the cautionary medical report, "A Man Who Pricked His Finger and Smelled Putrid for 5 Years."

1999 Dr. Arvid Vatle of Stord, Norway, for carefully collecting, classifying, and contemplating which kinds of containers his patients chose when submitting urine samples.

2000 Willibrord Weijmar Schultz, Pek van Andel, and Eduard Mooyaart of Groningen, the Netherlands, and Ida Sabelis of Amsterdam, for their illuminating report, "Magnetic Resonance Imaging of Male and Female Genitals During Coitus and Female Sexual Arousal."

2001 Peter Barss, of McGill University, for his impactful study "Injuries Due to Falling Coconuts."

2002 Chris McManus of UCL, England, for his excruciatingly balanced report, "Scrotal Asymmetry in Man and in Ancient Sculpture."

2003 Eleanor Maguire, David Gadian, Ingrid Johnsrude, Catriona Good, John Ashburner,

Continued on page 103

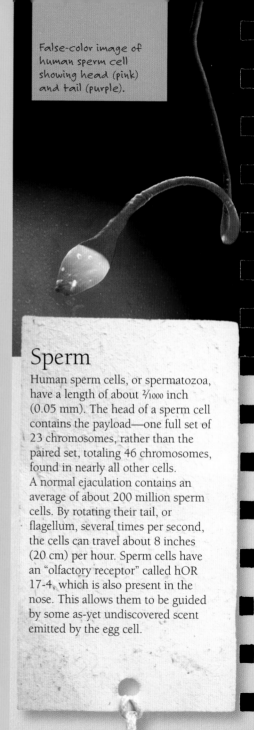

False-color image of human sperm cell showing head (pink) and tail (purple).

Sperm

Human sperm cells, or spermatozoa, have a length of about $\frac{2}{1000}$ inch (0.05 mm). The head of a sperm cell contains the payload—one full set of 23 chromosomes, rather than the paired set, totaling 46 chromosomes, found in nearly all other cells. A normal ejaculation contains an average of about 200 million sperm cells. By rotating their tail, or flagellum, several times per second, the cells can travel about 8 inches (20 cm) per hour. Sperm cells have an "olfactory receptor" called hOR 17-4, which is also present in the nose. This allows them to be guided by some as-yet undiscovered scent emitted by the egg cell.

Continued from page 102

Richard Frackowiak, and Christopher Frith of UCL, England, for presenting evidence that the brains of London taxi drivers are more highly developed than those of their fellow citizens.

2004 Steven Stack of Wayne State University, Detroit, Michigan, and James Gundlach of Auburn University, Auburn, Alabama, for their published report "The Effect of Country Music on Suicide."

2006 Francis M. Fesmire of the University of Tennessee College of Medicine, for his medical case report "Termination of Intractable Hiccups with Digital Rectal Massage"; and Majed Odeh, Harry Bassan, and Arie Oliven of Bnai Zion Medical Center, Haifa, Israel, for their subsequent medical case report also titled "Termination of Intractable Hiccups with Digital Rectal Massage."

2007 Brian Witcombe of Gloucester, England, and Dan Meyer of Antioch, Tennessee, for their penetrating medical report, "Sword Swallowing and Its Side Effects."

2008 Dan Ariely of Duke University, North Carolina, Rebecca L. Waber of MIT, Baba Shiv of Stanford University, and Ziv Carmon of INSEAD (Singapore) for demonstrating that high-priced fake medicine is more effective than low-priced fake medicine.

2009 Donald L. Unger, of Thousand Oaks, California, for investigating a possible cause of arthritis of the fingers, by diligently cracking the knuckles of his left hand—but never cracking the knuckles of his right hand—every day for more than 60 years. "Does Knuckle Cracking Lead to Arthritis of the Fingers?"

2010 Simon Rietveld of the University of Amsterdam, the Netherlands, and Ilja van Beest of Tilburg University, the Netherlands, for discovering that symptoms of asthma can be treated with a roller-coaster ride.

Body broker

Allen Tyler, once an employee at the University of Texas Medical Branch, was fired in 2002 after an audit revealed that he had made $18,000 from selling human fingernails and toenails to a company that used them in its research. He had stolen the nails from bodies that had been donated as "postmortem anatomical gifts." It is a federal crime to profit from the sale of body parts, and FBI investigations revealed that he had stolen and sold other body parts, including entire torsos and heads, earning more than $200,000 in all.

Every pint of your blood contains about 2½ ounces (70 g) of hemoglobin, packed into red blood cells; each hemoglobin molecule can carry four molecules of oxygen. Without hemoglobin, your blood could hold only about 1.5 ml of dissolved oxygen per pint (3 ml per liter). With it, your blood can carry up to 100 ml of oxygen per pint (200 ml per liter).

A world inside your wound

A remarkable chain of events takes place when you cut yourself. Bacteria enter the body through a break in the skin, filling the space around blood vessels. White blood cells called macrophages start to engulf the bacteria, while sending chemical requests for backup.

At the same time mast cells in the area release histamine, which increases blood flow to the wound site. This and the leakage of plasma into the space around the blood vessels cause the redness and swelling associated with inflammation. The swelling makes the injury increasingly painful. Histamine also causes small gaps to appear between the cells that make up the capillary walls near the injury.

Meanwhile, the backup arrives in the form of a crack team of assassins that pushes its way through the gaps—these neutrophil cells quickly begin destroying the invading bacteria. They can live for only a few hours outside blood vessels, and dead neutrophils begin to build up in the wound, giving pus its familiar yellow color.

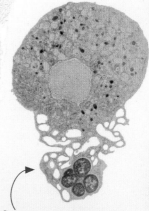

Bacteria (blue) trapped by a neutrophil (orange)

LET'S BEAT IT

According to the World Health Organization's International Agency for Research into Cancer, there were 12.7 million new cancer cases diagnosed and 7.6 million deaths worldwide in 2008. The most commonly diagnosed cancer was lung cancer, with 1.61 million cases (12.7 percent of the total). The next most common were breast cancer (1.38 million) and colorectal cancer (1.23 million).

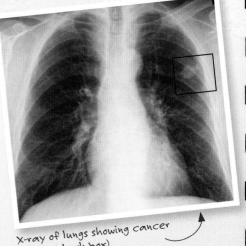

X-ray of lungs showing cancer (inside black box)

Oranges and lemons

The chemical name for vitamin C, ascorbic acid, comes from the Latin name for scurvy, *scorbutus*. This disease is caused by a deficiency of vitamin C, which the body does not make itself and so must obtain from the diet. Vitamin C plays a crucial role in the formation of collagen, which is a vital protein in many body tissues, including skin, bone, and blood vessels.

People suffering from scurvy experience pain in joints and muscles, red rashes around hair follicles, hair loss, unusual bleeding, and swollen, spongy, bleeding gums. It can be fatal if left untreated.

Although the disease was known in ancient times, scurvy became a significant problem when explorers began to make long sea voyages in the 15th and 16th centuries. Sailors had little or no access to sources of vitamin C on these journeys—since it is mostly present in fresh fruit and vegetables—and there was no way to keep them from perishing.

Scottish physician James Lind was the first to prove that citrus fruits cure scurvy, when he carried out the world's first real systematic clinical trial in 1747. Nevertheless, the problem persisted until World War I in the early 20th century.

GOOD SOURCES OF VITAMIN C

Baobab

Citrus fruits, such as oranges, grapefruit, lemons

Cruciferous vegetables, such as broccoli, Brussels sprouts, cabbage, cauliflower

Red and green peppers

Papayas

Soft fruit, such as strawberries, raspberries, blackcurrant, elderberry

Lychees   Potatoes

Melons   Tomatoes

Mangos   Liver

Spinach   Oysters

Garlic

Something missing

The retina is the light-sensitive surface at the back of the eye. Near the center of the retina, there is a small area that is not light-sensitive at all: it is the bit where the nerves from your retina bundle together to form the optic nerve. When both eyes are open, the brain gets information about that part of the visual field from the other eye. When you have just one eye open, your brain "fills in" the missing information. To see this for yourself, close your left eye and look at the cross (above); move your head closer and further away from the book and, at the right distance, the dot will disappear. But you won't see a "hole": your brain will fill in the empty space with the color of the background.

YOU CAN'T DO IT
Sit in a chair with your right foot off the ground and make it move in clockwise circles. Now, draw a figure six in the air with your right hand, while trying to keep your foot turning clockwise.

BLOODTHIRSTY AFTER THE EVENT

In 193 CE, Roman emperor Septimus Severus passed a decree banning a strange ritual that had become all too common: drinking the blood of dying gladiators. Ancient peoples had the idea that blood carried some kind of life force—and some of the physical and mental strength of the person whose blood it was. In this way of thinking, it seems quite reasonable to expect that drinking the blood of gladiators might help someone to become strong and brave.

Gladiator

LOW-DOWN

The suffix "hypo-" means below, beneath, or less than normal.

Hypoglycemia: Below normal blood sugar level.

Hypothalamus: The part of the brain just below the thalamus.

Hypodermic syringe: A needle for injecting medicines beneath the skin.

Hypotension: Below normal blood pressure.

Hypothyroidism: Below normal production of thyroid hormones.

Hypoxia: Below normal oxygen concentration in the blood.

Hypoesthesia: Below normal sensation of touch.

Hypochondria: Beneath the breastbone.

Hypothermia: Below normal body temperature.

Hypotrichosis: Below normal hair growth.

Hypokalemia: Below normal potassium concentration in the blood.

Hyponatremia: Below normal sodium concentration in the blood.

Hypovolemia: Below normal volume of blood.

Funny words

A person who is highly sensitive to tickling is said to be hypergargalesthesic. This odd word derives from the scientific word for tickling—gargalesis. Delicate stroking on some parts of the body induces another type of tickling—normally unaccompanied by laughter, but accompanied by a shiver and an itch—which is called knismesis. And no, science has still not worked out why we cannot tickle ourselves.

The word "hypochondria" gave rise to the name of a state of mind in which a person is excessively worried about their health because of the ancient belief that melancholy originates in the organs of the abdomen, beneath the breastbone. The Greek word for the area below the breastbone is "hupokhondria."

The scientific term for low output of urine is oliguria. Pass no urine at all, and you have anuria.

Oil on canvas of Antonio López de Santa Ana on display in Mexico City Museum.

Phineus Gage with the tamping rod that injured him.

In 1838, the Mexican general Antonio López de Santa Ana held an elaborate state funeral for his leg, which was amputated after his ankle was shattered in battle.

The perils of gunpowder

In 1848, railway engineer Phineas Gage lost a significant part of his brain in an accident—but lived a normal life for another 12 years. Gage sustained horrific injuries in an accident while he was working on the construction of a railway track outside the town of Cavendish, Vermont. The accident happened as he was compacting gunpowder into a hole in a rock face with a long metal bar called a tamping rod. The gunpowder exploded, sending the rod through his skull and his brain at high speed.

The rod landed about 80 feet (25 m) away and was bloody and covered with bits of Gage's brain. The rod had entered Gage's head just below his left eye, passed through and destroyed the frontal lobe of his brain, and exited through the top of his skull.

Amazingly, Gage was speaking and walking around within a few minutes of the accident. Surgeons examining Gage shortly after could see his brain pulsing through his shattered skull. Within a year, Gage was more or less back to full health, with no pain in his head—although he described feeling a bit strange.

WHAT IS CRAMP?

Painful muscle cramp can be caused simply by fatigue from over-exertion—in which case, massage and gentle stretching will help to relieve it. But often it is caused by a low level of three minerals: magnesium, calcium, and potassium. Eating foods rich in these minerals—such as bananas, peaches, cheese, chocolates, and seafood—can help to make cramps less likely. During exercise, isotonic drinks help to maintain levels of these minerals lost through sweating.

The world's first atomic artillery shell, the Grable shell, detonates in the Nevada test site, in May 1953.

THE BONE SEEKER

The bones and teeth of everyone on Earth almost certainly contain detectable amounts of the element strontium-90. Naturally occurring strontium (strontium-84) is harmless, but strontium-90 is radioactive: it is produced in fission reactions, in nuclear reactors, and nuclear weapons. Most of the strontium-90 in people around the world comes from the fallout from above-ground nuclear weapons tests.

Too much strontium-90 can cause bone cancer and leukemia. But for most people, the presence of atoms of this unnatural isotope poses little risk. There is significantly more strontium-90 in people born between 1945, the year of the first nuclear weapons test, and 1963, when a test ban treaty stopped most countries from testing above ground.

Hormones? Yeah, right! Whatever!

Puberty's puppet master

Puberty is a time of great upheaval in the body. It all begins with a compound called gonadotropin releasing hormone (GnRH). This hormone is almost completely absent in early childhood. When the hypothalamus begins producing GnRH—at about age 10 in girls and 12 in boys—everything changes. When receptors for GnRH in the pituitary gland detect the new hormone, they start producing the two gonadotropin hormones: follicle stimulating hormone (FSH) and luteinizing hormone (LH).

FSH causes sex cells—eggs and sperm—to develop. LH causes boys' testes to produce testosterone. In girls, a distinct rise in LH production once a month stimulates ovulation and stimulates the production of a structure in the ovaries called the corpus luteum, which itself produces progesterone and other hormones necessary for maintaining a pregnancy. The hypothalamus delivers GnRH in pulses, with one burst every two or three hours. In boys, the pulses are regular, but in girls, the frequency varies. More frequent pulses stimulate the production of LH, less frequent ones, FSH.

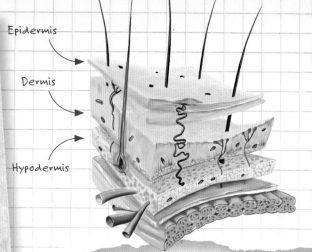

Epidermis

Dermis

Hypodermis

A goiter is a swelling in the neck, caused by an enlargment of the thyroid gland. The most common cause is iodine deficiency.

YOUR OWN PERSONAL COUNTERWEIGHT

Your buttocks act as a counterweight: you automatically move them backward to help keep your balance when you are bending forward. To see how important this is, stand with your heels against a wall and try bending forward to touch the ground. You will fail forward, so please be careful!

What a big organ

The biggest organ of your body is … your skin. An organ is a grouping of cells that serve a common purpose and, on average, the skin accounts for about 16 percent of our body weight. It is remarkable stuff: it protects us from toxic substances, ultraviolet radiation, heat, and microorganisms; it provides a huge area for sensing the outside world, via nerve endings; and when exposed to sunlight, it produces vitamin D. Skin is about ½₅ inch (1 mm) thick and has three layers: the epidermis, dermis, and hypodermis.

The **epidermis** is outermost. Its cells make keratin, a tough protein, and melanin, a pigment that gives skin its color. Over about 30 days, skin cells move up through the epidermis, eventually dying and being shed.

The **dermis** contains the proteins collagen and elastin, which make the skin strong and elastic. It is also the location of hair roots, sweat glands, and nerve endings that sense heat and pressure.

Some of these nerve endings are also found in the bottom layer, the **hypodermis**, which is mostly fatty tissue threaded with blood and lymph vessels. The fat is called subcutaneous ("under the skin").

FLABs—FOUR-LETTER ABBREVIATIONS

ACTH Adrenocorticotropic hormone

ADHD Attention deficit hyperactivity disorder

AIDS Acquired immune deficiency syndrome

CAIS Complete androgen insensitivity syndrome

COPD Chronic obstructive pulmonary disease

DHEA Dehydroepiandrosterone

ESRD End stage renal disease

fMRI Functional magnetic resonance imaging

GHRH Growth hormone-releasing hormone

MRSA Methicillin-resistant *Staphylococcus aureus*

NADH Nicotinamide adenine dinucleotide

SARS Severe acute respiratory syndrome

SSRI Selective serotonin reuptake inhibitor

SSSS Staphylococcal scalded skin syndrome

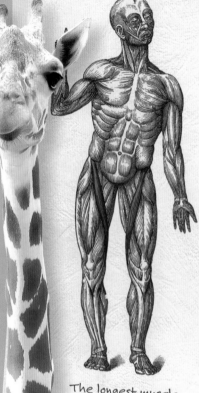

The longest muscle in the body is the sartorius, which winds around the femur (thigh bone). One end is connected to the hip, the other to the knee.

Giraffe neck

The long and short of it

Your neck has seven vertebrae—and so does a giraffe's neck, despite the fact that a giraffe can stand up to 19 feet (6 m) tall, with a neck as long as 6 feet 6 inches (2 m). As the giraffe's neck developed through evolution, the bones gradually became elongated.

Human neck

Bodies of the Solar System

SKELETON OF NICOLAUS COPERNICUS—DIED 1543

Polish astronomer Nicolaus Copernicus formulated the theory that the Sun is at the center of the Solar System. He was buried in an unmarked grave beneath a cathedral in the Polish city of Frombork—and his remains lay there anonymously for more than 460 years, until they were discovered in 2005. In 2008, scientists proved that the bones belonged to Copernicus by comparing their DNA with DNA from a hair found in one of his books. Copernicus was finally reburied in 2010, after the skull had been used to produce a three-dimensional model of the astronomer's head.

Galileo on a 1983 2,000-lire banknote from Italy

FINGER OF GALILEO GALILEI—DIED 1642

Italian astronomer, physicist, and mathematician Galileo Galilei was one of the most prolific and important scientists of all time. His astronomical observations, using the newly invented telescope, gave support to Copernicus' theory. More than 90 years after his death, Galileo's body was exhumed—during the exhumation, his finger was snapped off. Galileo's finger is now on permanent display in the Museo Galileo, Florence, Italy.

SKELETON OF TYCHO BRAHE—DIED 1601

Danish astronomer Tycho Brahe made the most accurate astronomical observations of his time, which provided much support to Copernicus' theory. In 1901—exactly 300 years after his death—Tycho's body was exhumed from his grave in Prague, Czechoslovakia (now the Czech Republic). It is possible that mercury poisoning contributed to his death, as high levels of this toxic metal were found when his body was exhumed again in 2010.

DEATH MASK OF ISAAC NEWTON—DIED 1727

Newton was an English physicist, mathematician, and astronomer whose theory of gravity helped to prove Copernicus' theory. After his death, several plaster-cast death masks of his face were made. Some are still in existence, including one at Trinity College at the University of Cambridge, England, where Newton studied and later taught.

Isaac Newton's death mask

Foods to look out for

Carrots are a good source of vitamin A, which is essential for proper vision. Vitamin A forms a compound called retinal, a light-sensitive molecule at the heart of vision. Vitamin A is available in other orange vegetables, including sweet potatoes and pumpkin, and in orange fruits such as apricots, mangoes, and peaches. Milk, eggs, and liver are other good sources. Deficiency of this vital vitamin is the biggest cause of blindness in developing countries.

Another important vegetable to include in a "vision diet" is spinach. It contains plenty of lutein, which is a yellow pigment found in the retina. Lutein, together with another yellow pigment called zeaxanthin, are found in the macula—the part of the retina most densely packed with light-sensitive cells. These pigments absorb harmful ultraviolet light, protecting the macula from damage. One in six people over 60, and one in three people over 70, suffer with sight loss through a disease called age-related macular degeneration. Plenty of lutein in your diet—available in broccoli, egg yolk, peas, Brussels sprouts, and kale—can help to prevent or slow down this disease.

Spinach

CAN A RUSTY NAIL GIVE YOU TETANUS?

Tetanus, formerly known as "lockjaw," is a potentially fatal disease caused by a bacterium called *Clostridium tetani*. This bacterium thrives in deep wounds because it is anaerobic—it prefers environments with little oxygen. A rusty nail may have been outside long enough to have probably picked up the bacterium, which commonly lives in soil—but a cut from a rusty nail is otherwise no more likely to cause tetanus than any other wound.

Forbidden fruit?

In case you have never stopped to think about it, the Adam's apple is called that in reference to the story of Adam and Eve, from the Book of Genesis in the Old Testament of the Bible. In the story, Adam ate the fruit of the tree of knowledge of good and evil. A popular interpretation of the story, in the Christian tradition at least, is that the forbidden fruit was an apple, and that it "got stuck in Adam's throat." In an informal sense, this would explain why the Adam's apple is more prominent in men than in women. The Adam's apple is made of the cartilage that contains and supports the larynx, or voice box—its proper name is the "laryngeal prominence."

Interestingly, the Book of Genesis does make a reference to anatomy—in a way that creates some confusion among some people. It states that Eve was created from one of Adam's ribs. As a result, some people believe that women have one more pair of ribs than men—in fact, men and women both have twelve pairs.

Adam's
apple

NAKED BITS
Skin that is devoid
of hair—on the
underside of
fingers, the palms,
the soles of the
feet, and the lips,
labia minora, and
penis—is called
glabrous skin.

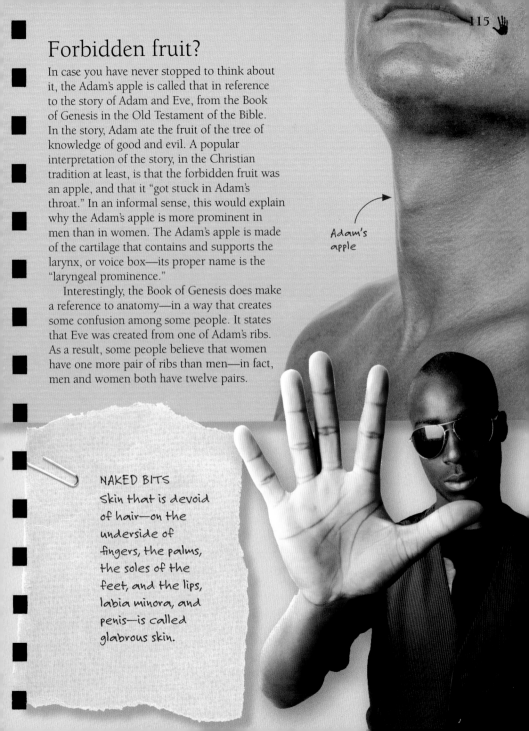

Hmmm. I wonder how much broccoli it will take to turn my urine green?

Flaying alive, flaying alive

Until the 16th century, it was very uncommon to peel the skin away from (flay) a human body, dead or alive. In that century, it became fairly common, as interest in and understanding of anatomy and physiology gathered pace. For a time, it was very fashionable for art and anatomy textbooks to feature images of flayed bodies.

There was a flaying that many people had been aware of for many centuries before—albeit a fictional one. Marsyas, a satyr (flute player) in ancient Greek mythology, was flayed alive after he had challenged the god Apollo to a musical duel on a double-piped flute and lost. Roman poet Ovid described the scene in *Metamorphoses*, written in the 1st century CE:

The Fate of Marsyas
Scarce had the man this famous story told,
Of vengeance on the Lycians shown of old,
When strait another pictures to their view
The Satyr's fate, whom angry Phoebus slew;
Who, rais'd with high conceit, and puff'd with pride,
At his own pipe the skilful God defy'd.
Why do you tear me from my self, he cries?
Ah cruel! must my skin be made the prize?
This for a silly pipe? he roaring said,
Mean-while the skin from off his limbs was flay'd.
All bare, and raw, one large continu'd wound,
With streams of blood his body bath'd the ground.
The blueish veins their trembling pulse disclos'd,
The stringy nerves lay naked, and expos'd;
His guts appear'd, distinctly each express'd,
With ev'ry shining fibre of his breast.

GREEN, BUT NOT WITH ENVY

Broccoli was a very popular food in ancient Rome. It was the favorite food of Drusus Caesar, the son of the Roman emperor Tiberius: he ate almost nothing else for more than a month. His father ordered him to stop when his urine began to come out green, and his skin took on a greenish hue. He died aged 36, and so did not really benefit from eating so much broccoli: its many health benefits include being a rich source of sulforaphane, a compound that has promising anticancer and antibacterial properties.

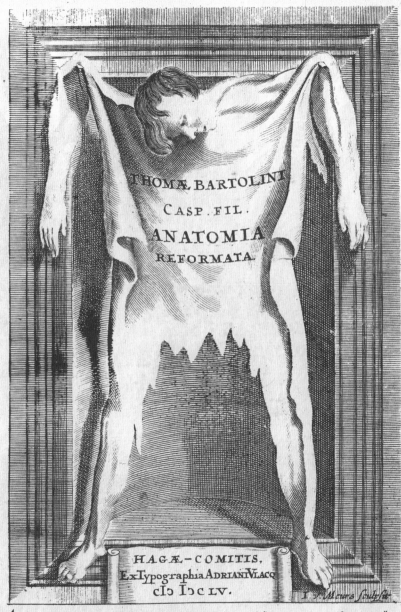

THOMÆ BARTOLINI

CASP. FIL.

ANATOMIA

REFORMATA.

HAGÆ–COMITIS,
Ex Typographia ADRIANI VLACQ
cIↃ IↃc LV.

This image is the gruesome frontispiece of "Anatomica Reformata"
(1655), written by influential anatomist Thomas Bartholin, who
famously discovered the lymphatic system.

Palpating the
abdomen of a
trauma patient.

When a doctor presses his or
her fingers into your abdomen
or your chest to feel for
swelling, or a midwife feels a
pregnant woman's abdomen
to check the baby, they are
said to be "palpating." The
word comes from the Latin
word "palpare," which means
"to feel"—and which is the
root of the word "palpable."

What type of hair?

There are three types of hair that
grow on the body (as opposed to
the head):

1. Lanugo hair: Fine and downy,
covers developing fetuses, usually lost
before birth.

2. Vellus hair: Soft, short, fair, and
fluffy, found all over the body.

3. Terminal hair: Long, thick, and
normally dark. In some parts of the
body, such as the armpits and pubic
area, vellus hair becomes terminal
at puberty.

A STITCH IN TIME
No one really knows the cause
of a stitch—the pain in the
side often felt by long-
distance runners. There are
two main theories: one, that
it is caused by cramp in the
diaphragm, and two, that
liquids in the intestines tug
on the ligaments connecting
to the diaphragm.

Womb with a view

Louise Brown, the first "test-tube baby," conceived by *in vitro* fertilization (IVF), was born on July 25, 1978, in Oldham, England. Since then more than one million babies conceived using IVF have been born.

A substance that increases the production of saliva is called a ptyalagogue, or alternatively a sialagogue.

An embryologist transferring an egg to a special culture media in a petri dish.

"Sternutation"—from the Latin "sternutare," which means "to spread out or scatter"—is another word for sneezing.

> I'm creating my own little carbon store.

CARBON MOUTHPRINT

An adult produces an average of more than $\frac{1}{100}$ ounce (0.5 g) of carbon dioxide every minute, which he or she breathes out. This amounts to nearly 2 pounds (1 kg) per day—but since the source of the carbon is food, a renewable energy source, it does not contribute directly to climate change.

BLADDER OF SUCCESS

In 2006, scientists grew human bladders in the laboratory, and successfully transplanted them into seven patients—the first artificial organ transplants in humans. The bladders were grown from cells taken from the patients' own, damaged, bladders, so there was no chance of their bodies rejecting the implant.

Do you copy?

In 2002, Bahamas-based company Clonaid made a very public claim that they had carried out the world's first human reproductive cloning—and that a baby, named Eve, had been born as a result. The company has close ties with a "UFO religion" called Raëlism, which believes that life on Earth was created by intelligent extraterrestrial beings. Clonaid has since claimed that it has carried out several other successful cloning attempts—but no proof has ever been offered, and the scientific community considers the claims as nothing more than a publicity stunt.

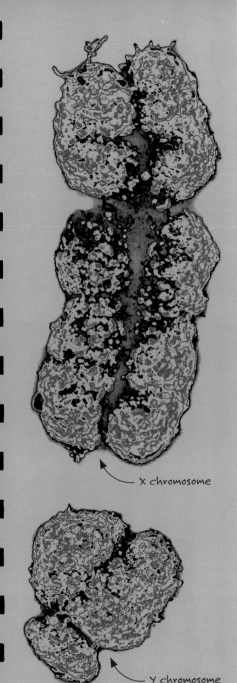

X chromosome

Y chromosome

Sex chromosomes

The sex of a baby is determined at conception by the combination of sex chromosomes in the fertilized egg. There are two different types: X chromosomes and Y chromosomes. Nearly everyone inherits one sex chromosome from the mother and one from the father: the chromosome from the mother is always an X chromosome, and that from the father may be either an X or a Y chromosome. An X-X combination produces a female child, an X-Y combination a male. Note that Y-Y is not possible, since the sex chromosome inherited from the mother is always an X. However, there are rare cases in which a baby inherits one, three, or four sex chromosomes instead of the standard two. Scientists' shorthand for a person's set of chromosomes involves the total number of chromosomes present and the identities of the sex chromosomes; a "normal" male is characterized as 46,XY, a "normal" female as 46,XX.

45,X *Turner Syndrome*: Sex organs don't mature at adolescence, infertility, short stature, often a "webbed" neck.

47,XXY, 48,XXYY or 48,XXXY *Klinefelter's Syndrome*: Males, normally with reduced fertility and small genitalia, and often with enlarged breast tissue.

47,XXX *Triple X Syndrome*: Normally few symptoms, since only one X chromosome is activated, even in normal females.

47,XYY *XYY Syndrome*: Tend to have no physical symptoms, but often some learning difficulties.

A tattoo design on the back of a young woman.

A brush with life

Several scientific studies have concluded that regular brushing, and good general dental hygiene, can reduce your risk of cardiovascular disease (heart attack and stroke)—even after accounting for other factors, such as diet and smoking. What could be behind this strange connection? Bad dental hygiene can lead to bleeding gums, which allow the most common oral bacteria, *Streptococcus*, into the blood. These cunning microorganisms then fool blood platelets into forming a defensive shield around them—a mini blood clot. This clot can block an artery, but it can also produce a sustained inflammatory response. In the blood vessels, this response can accelerate the formation of atherosclerosis, commonly known as hardening of the arteries—the biggest cause of cardiovascular disease.

In 1922, 28-year-old Charles Osborne, from Anthon, Iowa, began hiccuping while he was weighing a hog. He hiccuped continuously from then until 1990, making his the longest-known attack of hiccups in history.

PERMANENT FIXTURE

Tattoos do not rub off, despite the fact that we are continuously shedding and renewing our skin. This is because the dyes used in the procedure become encapsulated by "fibroblasts"—cells that form connective tissue to repair damaged skin. A tattoo artist injects the dye into the dermis, which is composed of living tissues, not the epidermis (outermost layer), which is mostly made of dead cells ready to flake off.

The Omo Kibish site is an ancient rocky formation near the town of Kibish in southern Ethiopia, and is the location of the archaeology dig where human bones believed to be 195,000 years old were discovered along the Omo River.

Old bones

Human bones discovered between 1967 and 1974 in the Omo National Park in Ethiopia, are the oldest-known specimens of anatomically modern humans ever found. The remains have been dated as 195,000 years old. Modern humans—the species called *Homo sapiens sapiens*—evolved from a number of older species, all now extinct.

A photograph of a physical slice through the frozen head of a male

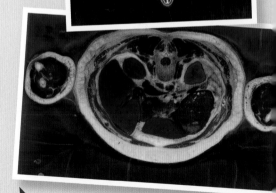

BEST THING SINCE SLICED BREAD

In 1989, the U.S. National Library of Medicine launched the Visible Human Project, which aims to build up a comprehensive database of anatomical imagery of a normal male and female human body. The imagery consists of "slices" through the bodies using CT (computed tomography), MRI (magnetic resonance imaging), and photographs of physical slices through a male and a female frozen body. Similar projects include the Visible Korean and the Chinese Visible Human.

A photograph of a physical slice through the frozen torso and arms of a female

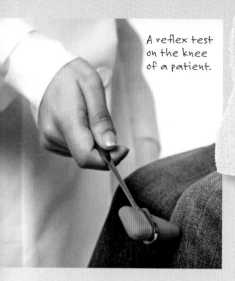

A reflex test on the knee of a patient.

The word "glaucoma" comes from the Greek word "glaukos," meaning blue-gray; people suffering from glaucoma often have a blue or grayish tinge in the lens and cornea of their eyes.

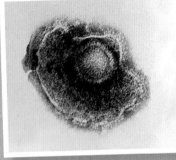

The chickenpox virus

Don't overstretch yourself

All muscles contain structures called spindles, which act as stretch sensors. When you lift a cup, your biceps (the muscle in the front upper arm) contracts, raising your lower arm. On the other side of the arm, your triceps stretches to allow the biceps to contract. As soon as it stretches, spindles in the triceps send a signal to the spinal cord; within a millisecond, the triceps muscle receives a signal back and it contracts, too. This "stretch reflex" helps to keep movements smooth and controlled and prevents muscles from becoming overstretched. If a doctor tests your reflexes by tapping a reflex hammer just beneath your kneecap, a tendon tugs on the quadriceps muscle in the thigh, causing it to stretch. In reflex, the muscle contracts or twitches, lifting the lower leg slightly.

DISEASES CAUSED BY HERPES VIRUSES

Herpesviridae is the name of a family of closely related viruses, more commonly known as herpes viruses. It includes herpes simplex viruses (HSV), the varicella zoster virus (VZV), the Epstein-Barr virus (EBV), and the Roseolovirus (HHV-6).

- Facial herpes (cold sores)—HSV
- Genital herpes—HSV
- Shingles—VZV
- Chickenpox—VZV
- Whitlow—HSV
- Roseola—HHV-6
- Mono (infectious mononucleosis, or glandular fever)—EBV

Six-banded armadillo

WHEN THE FEELING'S GONE AND YOU CAN'T GO ON

Leprosy is an infectious disease caused by bacteria. The myth that leprosy causes parts of the body to disintegrate and fall off arose because the disease often causes a numbness in the hands and feet that can lead to accidental burning or mutilation. The first effective vaccine for leprosy was developed in the 1980s, by taking blood products from infected armadillos—one of the very few animals that can develop the disease.

The word "callipygian" means "having finely developed buttocks."

MONDAY

18

I don't like Mondays

Several studies, in several different countries, have found that the risk of dying from a heart attack is significantly higher on a Monday than on any other day of the week. The reason may simply be the stress associated with returning to work—but evidence in one study suggested that increased drinking at the weekend might be an important factor.

WHAT IS THIS?

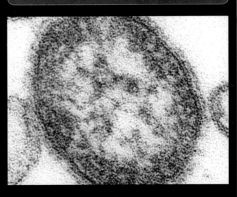

Answers on page 186.

Arms up

Stand in a doorway with your arms at your sides. Raise your arms and push the backs of your hands outward against the doorframe. Push as hard as you can and count to 30. Now step out of the doorway, stand still, and relax with your arms by your side. You should find that your arms rise involuntarily (if not, try again, but push harder and count for longer). In 2009, scientists discovered that this effect involves the part of the brain called the cerebellum, which helps adjust behavior to new conditions—in this case, the fact that the muscles have to push outward just to stay still. Don't worry—you'll find out the effect soon wears off.

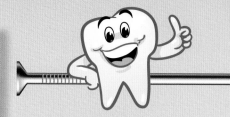

TOOTH AND NAIL

Tooth enamel is the hardest substance in the human body—harder (but not stronger) than a steel nail: on the Mohs scale of hardness, enamel has a value of 5 and steel 4.5. More than 95 percent of tooth enamel is mineral—mostly a substance called hydroxylapatite, which is also plentiful in bones. The mineral is built on a framework of proteins, but enamel is not a living tissue and has no blood supply or nerves of its own.

RELAXIN IN PREGNANCY

One of the main roles of a hormone called relaxin is to allow the pubic bones to widen during pregnancy. It does this by softening the piece of cartilage between the bones, called the pubic symphysis. Most of a woman's relaxin is produced by her ovaries and by breast tissue, but when a woman is pregnant, the placenta produces some, too. Relaxin is also produced in men: it is found in semen, where it increases the motility (ability to move) of sperm.

I'm just relaxin'.

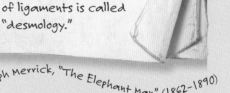

The scientific study of ligaments is called "desmology."

Joseph Merrick, "The Elephant Man" (1862–1890)

Dark chocolate

DOUBLE TROUBLE

The Englishman Joseph Merrick—commonly known as "The Elephant Man"—probably had a combination of two genetic diseases: Proteus syndrome and neurofibromatosis. These two rare conditions involve uncontrolled cell growth, leading to large tumors and skin and bone deformities. Merrick became well known in London after he was exhibited in a traveling "freak show." Merrick died in his sleep in 1890, aged 27.

The average adult human body contains about 0.12 g of lead—enough to make a cube slightly bigger than a large grain of sugar.

Actual size

Choca block

A 2010 Swedish study found that eating dark chocolate blocks the action of an enzyme called ACE (angiotensin-converting enzyme), which has been linked to increased rates of heart disease. Previous studies had shown that eating dark chocolate that has a high cocoa content was associated with reduced risk of heart disease, but the mechanism was not known. Dark chocolate also contains compounds called flavonoids, which have been shown to reduce blood cholesterol levels, another risk factor for heart disease.

Arm wrestling

Electroactive polymers (EAPs) are plastic materials that respond to an electric current by shrinking. They are a hot topic of research in robotics and prosthetics—they hold great promise for use as artificial muscles and would be a more natural and less "mechanical" option than the pneumatic or motor-driven artificial muscles used today. In 1999, NASA physicist Yoseph Bar-Cohen posed a challenge to EAP researchers: develop a robot arm using EAPs that can beat any human at arm wrestling. In March 2005, the first competition saw three robot arms thoroughly beaten, by a 17-year-old female student; it is still early days in EAP research.

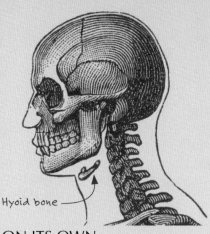

Hyoid bone

ON ITS OWN

The hyoid bone, which sits in the neck halfway between the Adam's apple and the lower jaw, is the only bone in the body that is not joined to at least one other bone. It provides a solid foundation for the movement of the tongue.

Arm wrestling with another human is a bit more difficult.

Muscles cannot push—they can only pull because they contract when activated.

YOUR BODY NEEDS ...

... chromium

The human body contains a tiny amount of chromium—about 14 mg, and the daily requirement is measured in millionths of a gram. But this metallic element is essential nonetheless, in the chemical reactions that process carbohydrates, fats, and proteins.

Foods that are good sources of chromium include brewer's yeast, beef, liver, broccoli, potatoes, garlic, and grapes.

Grapes are a good source of chromium.

I give you my heart

The earliest recorded tale of human organ transplantation dates back 2,500 years. Writing in about 350 BCE, Chinese Taoist sage Lieh Tsu recorded an account of a legendary swapping of hearts between two soldiers that reportedly took place about 150 years earlier. He wrote that the procedure was performed while the patients were in a "deathlike" state after drinking strong wine. The physician said to have carried out the transplant, Pien Ch'iao, had diagnosed one soldier as having strong mental powers but a weak will, and the other as having the opposite traits. Lieh Tsu wrote that the men were "as good as new" when they woke up—but this is very unlikely.

DEATH ON AN ENORMOUS SCALE

About 10 million cells in your body die in the time it takes you to read this sentence. But this is only one out of every 50 million or so. About 9 out of 10 of the cells that die are red blood cells, which are constantly renewed.

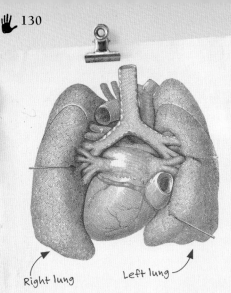

Right lung

Left lung

The left lung is slightly smaller than the right lung, to make room for the heart, which sits slightly left of center.

TAKE FOUR TISSUES

Connective tissue: This includes the tissues that make up the lower layers of the skin, the tendons and ligaments, cartilage, bone, and fat.

Epithelial tissue: The outer layer of the skin, the outer layer of internal organs, and the mucous membranes lining the mouth, stomach, and intestines.

Muscle tissue: Cardiac muscle (heart); smooth muscle, such as in the wall of the stomach and intestines; and skeletal muscles, such as the biceps.

Nervous tissue: Neurons, which process and transmit impulses; and glial cells, which support the neurons.

Sting in the (old wives') tale

Stinging nettle

The age-old European folklore remedy of rubbing dock leaves on the painful rash caused by stinging nettles actually provides no real relief: there are no compounds that could counteract the venom released by the trichomes (tiny hairs) on a nettle's leaves and stems. The act of rubbing may distract a child from the pain, however, and if the leaves are cool, then they may soothe the area. In fact, rubbing with a dock leaf could make the sting worse, by agitating any little hairs that have become lodged under the skin.

DNA "fingerprints" such as these are a standard part of forensic procedures around the globe. Generally, less than 0.1% of DNA differs between individuals.

DNA whodunnit?

DNA fingerprinting, also known as DNA profiling, was invented in 1984 by British geneticist Alec Jeffreys. The first time it was used in a criminal investigation, in 1986, it exonerated the main suspect in a brutal double murder—and in 1987 it identified the real perpetrator in the same case. The technique involves enzymes that cut DNA into pieces at specific points; the resulting tiny fragments are sorted by length in a special gel, resulting in a "profile" that looks somewhat like a bar code.

BREAKING THE FALL

The most commonly broken bone in the body is the collar bone, or clavicle. When people take a tumble, they instinctively hold their arms out in front of them, in order to break their fall. The impact transfers up the bones of the arm and causes a jolt to the collar bone. When it breaks, it normally does so about halfway from the shoulder to the breastbone, at its weakest point.

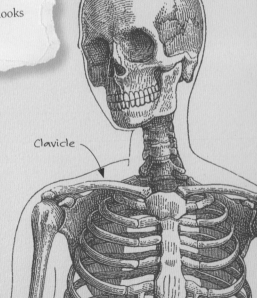

Clavicle

Cells in the bone marrow are replaced more quickly than those in any other tissue of the body.

I thought you were supposed to be the smart one!

Desperate measures

Under normal conditions, the brain uses only glucose as a fuel. It has no way of storing glucose and so needs a constant supply from carbohydrates in the diet. When the glucose that is immediately available runs out, the body turns to its carbohydrate store— reserves of glycogen found mostly in the liver. If the body receives no more food for a day or more, the glycogen store becomes depleted.

When this happens, the brain begins to take energy from small molecules called ketone bodies, derived from fatty acid molecules. (They give a fruity aroma to a person's breath.) If fasting continues for several days, the body will start breaking down proteins into amino acids, which are then converted into glucose in the liver. This is the last resort, because it involves the body literally "wasting away"—it is the equivalent of keeping warm by dismantling your house and burning the pieces on the fire.

I HATE CALCULUS

The scientific name for the brown staining on teeth more commonly known as tartar is "calculus." The name comes from the fact that tartar is formed by calcification of plaque, during which deposited minerals, predominantly calcium, cause the plaque to harden. Calculus has a rough texture, which provides an excellent location for more plaque to move in. Plaque is the film of bacteria that builds up on teeth and causes decay and gum disease. When plaque becomes hard, it is not easily removed by brushing.

The total length of all the blood vessels in your body is about 60,000 miles (100,000 km). Capillaries account for the vast majority of that length. Although each capillary is very short, there about 19 billion of them.

FACE FACTS

There are 14 bones in your face:

Inferior nasal concha × 2

Lacrimal bone × 2

Mandible × 1

Maxilla × 2

Nasal bone × 2

Palatine bone × 2

Vomer × 1

Zygomatic bone × 2

Lacrimal bone

Nasal bone

Vomer

Inferior nasal
concha is
hidden behind
the maxilla

Palatine bone
is the roof of
your mouth

Zygomatic bone

Maxilla

Mandible

Bloody cancer

Postmortem investigations of people who have died in car crashes found that about 40 percent of women in their 40s have microscopic tumors in their breasts, and about 50 percent of men in their 50s have microscopic tumors in their prostates. All cancers start out tiny—but they can grow only if they receive a blood supply. Once a tumor becomes established, new blood vessels also provide a route for more to spread around the body.

Research at the U.S.-based Angiogenesis Foundation has shown that preventing angiogenesis—the formation of new blood vessels—can be an effective medical treatment for cancer. They have also found that certain foods, such as fresh fruits and vegetables, contain naturally antiangiogenic compounds, which seem to help prevent cancer.

MOSTLY NONHUMAN

More than 90 percent of the cells in your body are nonhuman cells that belong to microbes. The Human Microbiome Project, run by the National Institutes of Health in the U.S.A., aims to identify all of those organisms that make their home in and on our bodies, and to find out more about how changes in the human ecosystem can cause disease.

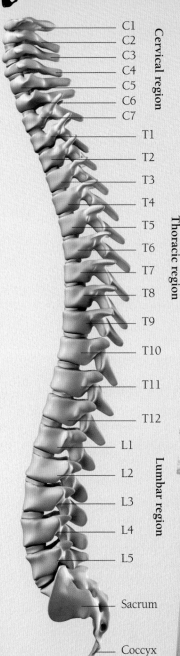

C1
C2
C3
C4
C5
C6
C7

Cervical region

T1
T2
T3
T4
T5
T6
T7
T8
T9
T10
T11
T12

Thoracic region

L1
L2
L3
L4
L5

Lumbar region

Sacrum

Coccyx

The spinal countdown

Anatomists divide the spine, or vertebral column, into three zones: cervical (neck), thoracic (back), and lumbar (lower back). There are a total of 24 movable vertebrae, numbered from upper through to lower within each zone. Below these movable vertebrae, there are five more that are movable only in childhood; these bones become fused together in adulthood, to form the sacrum. Below that is the coccyx, or tailbone, which is composed of a further four fused vertebrae.

A LIST FOR SORE EYES

Conditions that cause sore eyes:

- Acute glaucoma
- Allergies
- Inflammation of various parts of the eye, such as conjunctivitis, uveitis, scleritis, iritis, and blepharitis
- Smoke, dust, and foreign objects
- Entropion, in which the eyelid turns inward, causing the eyelashes to irritate the eye
- Ulcer on the cornea
- Eye muscle strain

Time to turn the other cheek.

Salpingo-oophorectomy is the name of the surgical procedure to remove both a fallopian tube and an ovary.

The probang is a flexible instrument used to treat the esophagus. These examples date from the 18th century.

Under pressure

Patients lying in bed for long periods have suffered from bedsores for as long as there have been beds. Over the years, many different remedies were used, including rubbing the oozing, open wounds with soap and methylated spirit. But none of these treatments was effective, with the result that these discharging wounds were often fatal. Bedsores, or pressure ulcers, are caused by the pressure of bones on the tissues of the skin, resulting in a reduced blood flow that kills the tissues. The heat and moisture trapped at the region of contact with the bed make the situation worse, and the skin and subcutaneous tissues become "macerated" (softened).

In the 1950s, English nurse Doreen Norton experimented with a new and extremely simple intervention: turning a patient every two hours relieves the pressure, massively reducing the incidence of bedsores. Norton's intervention heralded a new era in nursing and has saved many lives—although bedsores remain a major killer in many places in the world where this simple technique is not used.

DEEP IN THE THROAT

A probang is a long flexible rod, fitted with a small tuft of material, for removing obstructions from, or for applying medicine to, the esophagus (gullet) or trachea (windpipe).

The mucous cells lining the intestines are continuously renewed, each living for only a few days.

> **If the human brain were so simple that we could understand it, we would be so simple that we couldn't.**
>
> Emerson Pugh, computer scientist

Big babies, small babies

In developed countries, the average baby is born at "full term" (after 40 weeks' gestation), is about 20 inches (50 cm) long, and weighs between 6 and 9 pounds (2.7–4 kg). The averages are smaller in developing countries—and 100 years ago, average birthweight was around 7 ounces (200 g) less in developed countries, too.

Several babies have been born weighing less than 10 ounces (300 g), all of them several weeks premature. In 2004, probably the lightest baby ever to survive was born in Chicago. The girl weighed just 8.6 ounces (244 g)—less than a can of soft drink—and was just 8½ inches (24 cm) long. She was one of twins, born by cesarean section after only 25 weeks' gestation. Both twins survived and quickly put on weight.

Several babies have been born weighing more than 20 pounds (9 kg). The heaviest-known was a boy born in 1979 in Ohio; he weighed 23 pounds 12 ounces (10.8 kg). Sadly he died shortly after birth. His Canadian mother, Anna Bates, was herself an unusually large woman at 7 feet 5 inches (2.26 m) tall. The heaviest newborn baby to have survived is probably a boy born in 1955 in Aversa, Italy, who weighed in at 22 pounds 8 ounces (10.2 kg).

The average weight for healthy newborns is about 7 pounds (3.2 kg).

BLUE-BLOODED

The term "blue-blooded," meaning "aristocratic," originated in Spain in the 11th century. Arabs had occupied Spain for hundreds of years, but they were gradually displaced by people from Europe. The new ruling class had paler skin than most of the Arabs, so their blue veins were more visible.

Your body contains a total of about 45 miles (70 km) of sensory nerve fibers, which send impulses from their pressure-, heat-, or pain-sensing endings, which are mostly in the skin.

Your heart is about the size of your fist.

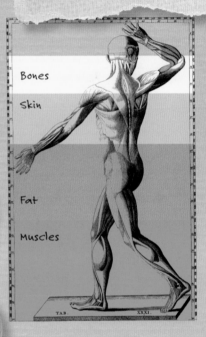

Bones

Skin

Fat

Muscles

TAB.   XXXI.

Muscles account for more than one-third of the average person's total body weight, fat around one-quarter, skin around one-sixth, and bones around one-eighth. More than half of the weight is made up by water, which is found throughout the body.

Invisible knowledge

An adult blinks an average of ten times every waking minute—that adds up to more than a quarter of a million times a year. Blinking happens less often when focusing on something, such as a book. During a blink, you lose sight of the world for nearly a third of a second; this means you completely miss several minutes of every feature film you see. Nevertheless, your brain is able to fill in the missing information and mostly manages to give the impression of continuous perception.

You also miss out on visual information every time your eyes flit from place to place when you turn your attention from one thing to another. These brief and speedy movements are called saccades, and your eyes perform them much more often than you realize. Just before a saccade, the brain suppresses its visual input, so that it will not "see" the blurred images during the tenth of a second or so it takes for the eye to move to its new position.

Flea

PASS IT ON

A zoonosis is any disease that humans can catch from nonhuman animals. Zoonoses that have become important in recent years include AIDS (acquired immune deficiency syndrome), bird flu, and swine flu. An important historical example is the plague, which was passed from rats to humans via fleas.

Stand in front of a mirror and look first at one eye and then at the other. You cannot see your eyes move—because of the suppression of the visual input to your brain during the saccade. But you do not notice a brief period of "nothingness"—because your brain "fills in" the missing images.

WHAT IS THIS?

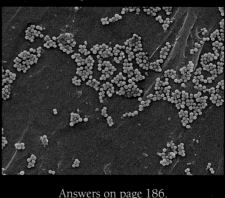

Answers on page 186.

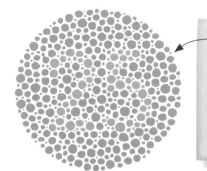

The first image in the Ishihara test for color blindness, which was designed in 1917 by Japanese ophthalmologist Shinobu Ishihara. Those with certain forms of color blindness will see a collection of random dots—everyone else will see the number 25. (Please note this image is for information purposes only—it cannot provide a medical diagnosis.)

COLOR BLINDNESS

We have millions of color-sensitive cells, called cones, in our eyes. There are three types, for seeing red, green, and blue light. The simplest form of color blindness is dichromatism, in which only two types of cone cell exist. There are three forms of this condition: protanopia (red cones missing), deuteranopia (green cones missing), and tritanopia (blue cones missing).

The most common forms of color blindness are called anomalous trichromacy. Here, all three types of receptors are present, but one type detects the wrong range of colors, due to a mutated gene. Again, there are three versions: protanomaly (mutated red cones), deuteranomaly (mutated green cones), and tritanomaly (mutated blue cones).

About 8 percent of males and only 0.5 percent of females are color blind. There is a simple reason for this: the genes for the red and green light-sensitive cone cells are found on the X chromosome. Males have only one X chromosome (and one Y), so if they have faulty versions of the genes, they will be affected. Females have two X chromosomes, so if they have at least one copy of each of the normal genes, they will not be red-green color blind.

BRAIN FREEZE

That short-lived headache you sometimes get if you eat very cold things is commonly known as a brain freeze—but the scientific term for it is "sphenopalatine ganglioneuralgia." When the roof of your mouth gets cold, your body reacts by dilating blood vessels, to bring more warm blood. This increase in blood flow to the head causes excess pressure, which is felt as a headache.

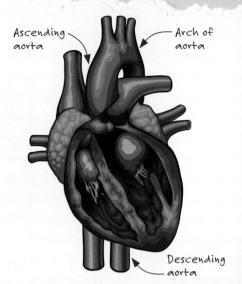

THE ACID TEST

In chemistry, pH is a measure of how acidic or alkaline a solution is. A "neutral" solution, that is neither acidic nor alkaline, has a pH value of 7. Acids have a pH less than 7, alkalis greater than 7.

Blood in arteries: pH 7.40

Blood in veins: pH 7.35

Urine: Average pH 6.00

Saliva: Normal range pH 6.00–7.40

Arterial blood with a pH of less than 7.35 is in a state of acidosis; with a pH above 7.45, it is in a state of alkalosis. Acidosis can cause shortness of breath, nausea, diarrhea, fatigue, and muscle spasm; alkalosis can cause muscle spasms, muscle weakness, and general irritability.

Ascending aorta

Arch of aorta

Descending aorta

Your inner hose

The aorta is the largest artery in the human body. The part that emerges from the heart—the ascending aorta—is about the size of a rather large garden hose: it has a diameter of just over 1 inch (about 3 cm). The main part of the artery is the descending aorta, which passes down through the abdomen; it is just less than 1 inch (about 2 cm) in diameter.

Blind to the facts

About 314 million people worldwide are visually impaired; 45 million of them are blind, and women are at much greater risk than men. Cataracts account for about 48 percent of all cases, despite the fact that they are easy to treat. A cataract occurs when the lens of the eye becomes clouded over, obstructing vision. The lens is made of water and proteins, and with age, disease, or trauma, the protein molecules can become denatured (lose some aspects of their structure), making the mixture opaque. A similar process happens to the proteins in egg white when you fry or boil an egg.

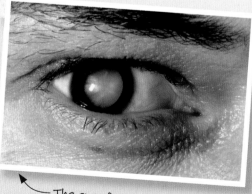

The eye of a male patient with a mature cataract.

BREATHLESS

At altitude, the air is "thinner" because its density and pressure decrease with increasing height. As the pressure of oxygen is reduced, less oxygen dissolves in the blood inside the lungs with each breath. Sensors in the neck called carotid bodies detect the low oxygen and send nerve impulses to a part of the brain called the medulla oblongata. This increases heart and breathing rates, to compensate. If you remain at high altitude for days and weeks, your body effects a number of longer-term physiological changes, called acclimatization, which increase the amount of oxygen in your blood. These changes include increasing the number and the individual mass of red blood cells and growing new capillaries in your muscles.

Ouch! My ...? Now what did they call it before I arrived?

Achilles' heel

The Achilles tendon, which joins three muscles to the heel bone, is named after mythological Greek hero Achilles. When he was a baby, Achilles' mother immersed him in the magical river Styx, to make his body invincible. But she missed out the part of his body with which she was holding him—his heel, which became his one vulnerability. In the Trojan War, Achilles was killed when an arrow pierced his heel.

Rapid response

Some nerves are insulated with a sheath of a fatty substance called myelin. Nerve impulses travel at around 3.3 feet per second (1 m/sec) in unmyelinated nerve fibers, and around 330 feet per second (100 m/sec), or 200 mph (360 kph), in myelinated ones. Myelin is essential to the proper functioning of neurons in the brain; the disease multiple sclerosis is the result of damage to and loss of myelin, known as demyelination.

Coral is sometimes used in bone grafts.

HARD GRAFT

More than a million bone grafts are performed worldwide every year to replace missing pieces of bones in people who have serious fractures. What sources do doctors use?

♥ The patient's own bone, taken from elsewhere in the body, typically the pelvis or the chin.

♥ Human bone from a dead donor, via a tissue bank.

♥ Coral, which has a similar structure and consistency to bone.

♥ Artificial bones, typically manufactured from minerals similar to those in real bone.

♥ Bones from other animals, most commonly cows.

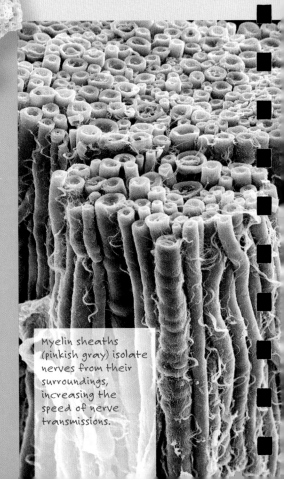

Myelin sheaths (pinkish gray) isolate nerves from their surroundings, increasing the speed of nerve transmissions.

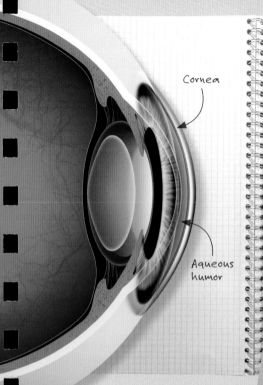

Cornea

Aqueous humor

BLOODLESS TISSUE

The cornea—the transparent outermost layer of the eyeball—is the only living tissue in the body that does not have blood vessels. It receives nutrients from tears and from the layer beneath it (the aqueous humor), and it receives oxygen directly from the air. The cornea does, however, have nerve endings: in fact, it is densely packed with nerves, making it one of the most sensitive parts of the human body.

The history of birth control begins in ancient Egypt, where women used crocodile dung as a spermicide.

Uses for(e) skin …

Whatever is your take on the ethics of infant circumcision, have you ever wondered what happens to all the leftover foreskins? The skin of an infant's foreskin is rich in keratinocytes, which produce keratin (the key structural material in skin), and fibroblasts, which produce collagen (the main structural protein in connective tissue). Research and cosmetics companies pay thousands of dollars for a single foreskin. Some foreskins are used to grow human skin cells for medical research, some are used to produce collagen for high-end face creams, and some are used to make skin grafts for burns victims.

Your eyes are streaming

Your eyes each send about 8.75 megabits of information to the brain every second, about the same as a decent broadband connection. The estimate comes from a study carried out in 2006, by researchers at the University of Pennsylvania in Philadelphia. The team measured the amount of information passing along the optic nerves of a guinea pig, then scaled the results up for humans, who have more light-sensitive cells in their retinas, but otherwise a very similar visual system.

The fluid in blisters at the site of a burn is rich in chemical messengers called angiogenic chemokines, which promote the development of new blood vessels. The more severe the burn, the more angiogenic chemokines present in the fluid.

Index finger (2D)

Ring finger (4D)

Man's hand

GOING DIGITAL

The ratio between the lengths of the index finger (the second digit, 2D) and the ring finger (4D) seems to depend upon our exposure to testosterone when in the womb. A male fetus produces lots of testosterone, while a female one does not; in males, the index finger is usually shorter than the ring finger; in females, the ring finger is usually shorter. The 2D:4D ratio is a "predictor" of many things, including a man's testicle size and sperm count; a man's likelihood of developing prostate cancer, and a woman's of developing breast cancer; the likelihood of developing autism; sporting ability; musical ability; exam success; and, in women, assertiveness.

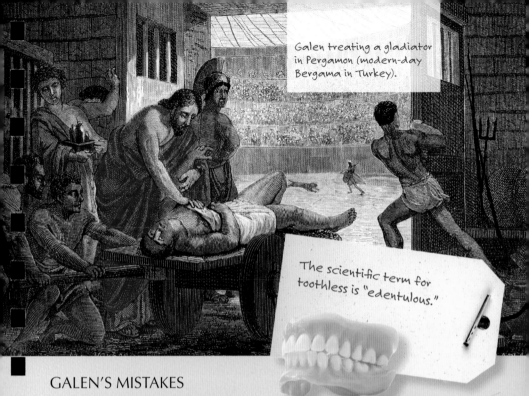

Galen treating a gladiator in Pergamon (modern-day Bergama in Turkey).

The scientific term for toothless is "edentulous."

GALEN'S MISTAKES

One of the most influential anatomists of the ancient world was Greek physician Claudius Galen, born in the year 129, who worked in Rome. Roman law at the time forbad him from using human cadavers in his anatomical studies. And so, although he carried out dissections nearly every day of his working life, he worked only on monkeys and apes, pigs, sheep, cows, dogs ,and, once, the Roman emperor's pet elephant. Being mammals, all of these animals have broadly similar anatomy to humans—but not identical. Also, Galen lived at a time when our understanding of biology and chemistry was very limited, and the microscope had not yet been invented. As a result, despite Galen's brilliance, he made many errors that were not picked up for more than a thousand years, including:

♥ He wrongly claimed that the human lower jaw is composed of two bones (there is only one).

♥ He wrongly believed that human breastbones are composed of seven bones (there are three).

♥ His anatomical understanding of the human womb was based on dogs.

♥ He positioned the kidneys in the same place as a pig's kidneys (too high).

♥ His detailed anatomy of the brain is based on work with cows.

♥ He believed that the liver transforms food into blood.

♥ He did not realize that blood circulates and that the heart is a pump.

THERE'S A GENE FOR THAT

Some surprising human traits are determined, at least in part, by specific genes. The scientific term for a particular version of a gene making something more likely is "predisposition." Whether a particular trait actually develops depends on many genes and on a person's environment and sometimes how they choose to live. So, while there is a "gene for alcoholism," it is merely the case that one version of that gene is more common in people addicted to alcohol—not that the gene "causes" alcoholism. Here is a very partial list of some genes that have been discovered:

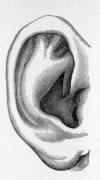

The outer part of the ear is called the pinna—it is mostly cartilage, and its job is to collect and amplify sound. The lobe is just the piece of skin at the bottom of the pinna—it contains no cartilage, which is why it is more floppy than the rest of the pinna.

Trait	Name of gene or genetic marker
Male homosexuality	Xq28
Left-handedness	LRRTM1
Ruthlessness	AVPR1A
Obesity	FTO (plus 41 others)
Alcoholism	GABRG3
Schizophrenia	WKL1
General intelligence (IQ)	CHRM2 (disputed)
Anxiety and aggression	PET-1
Curly hair	TCHH
Dry skin	R501X and 2284del4
Type 2 diabetes	HNF4
Hair loss	APCDD1

Pain in the head

Headaches are categorized using the International Classification for Headache Disorders (ICHD), which was created by the International Headache Society in 1988. Major groups of headache type include tension-type headaches (90 percent), sinus headaches, migraine, cluster, and hormone headaches, and oral-induced headaches.

YOUR BODY NEEDS ...

... selenium

An adult human body contains only about 15 mg of selenium; the bodies of about 70 people would be needed if you wanted to harvest 1 g of it. In large amounts, this little-known metallic element is extremely toxic—but as a trace mineral, it is vital for many bodily functions. It is present in some "selenoproteins" that function as antioxidant enzymes, destroying harmful substances called free radicals. It also plays an important role in the proper operating of the immune system and the thyroid gland. Selenium is found in two amino acids, which are the molecules that join together to make proteins, so it is found in protein-rich foods, including nuts, meat, fish, and eggs.

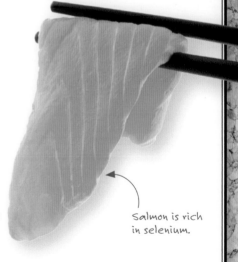

Salmon is rich in selenium.

They'll never know I'm a witch. Mine are warts not moles.

WAX ON, WAX OFF, HAIR OFF, SKIN OFF

Removing hair using hot wax can remove skin, too, if the wax is left on for too long. It can also cause inflammation of the hair follicles (folliculitis). As a result of admissions to hospital—and at least one lawsuit against a waxing spa—the State of New Jersey moved to ban so-called Brazilian waxing in 2009.

MOLES

- In 17th-century Europe, it was common to prick moles on the skin of a suspected witch. If the mole did not bleed, the person was held to be a witch—and put to death. (Some unscrupulous witch hunters had special retractable blades that would not even prick the skin.)

- One in about a hundred babies is born with a mole.

- The brown color of moles is due to the skin pigment melanin.

- Moles form from a proliferation of skin cells, and their particular color depends upon the layer of skin in which they form.

- Picking a mole will not cause cancer—but it could cause an infection, so don't do it.

- A small number of moles (typically the itchy, bleeding ones of irregular and changing shape) do go on to form malignant melanoma—a form of skin cancer.

- If a doctor has to remove a mole, he or she typically freezes it with liquid nitrogen then scrapes it away.

- Molemancy is the (nonscientific) divination of a person's character by looking at the position and characteristics of their moles.

Dwarf from Svaneti in the Eurasian country Georgia

About two out of every three cases of dwarfism are caused by a bone growth disorder called achondroplasia, which is normally due to a mutation caused during fertilization, rather than an inherited condition.

Kill the pain

Aspirin and ibuprofen are the most popular examples of a group of drugs called nonsteroidal anti-inflammatory drugs (NSAIDs). They both work in the same way, by inhibiting the action of enzymes called cyclooxygenases (COXs). These enzymes normally produce compounds called prostaglandins, which play an important role in the inflammation response and in sensing pain. Prostaglandins also control the body's temperature set-point, and inhibiting their production brings that set-point down, which can be useful in reducing fever. Another popular painkiller is acetaminophen; no one is completely sure of how it works, but there is evidence that it, too, inhibits the action of one of the COX enzymes.

Around 80% of osteoporosis sufferers are women.

A woman's eye with pupil dilated

REASONS WHY PUPILS DILATE ...

❦ Dim light

❦ The hormone epinephrine, in response, for example, to excitement, fear, or caffeine

❦ The hormone oxytocin, during sexual arousal

❦ Certain diseases, such as stroke and epilepsy

❦ Some illegal drugs, including LSD, cocaine, and heroin

❦ Mydriatic medications, such as tropicamide ("mydriasis" is the term for a pupil that remains dilated)

❦ Head injury

❦ Death

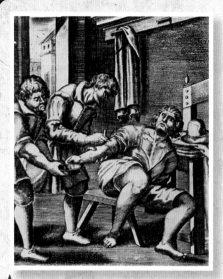

Bleeding outdated?

From ancient times until the 19th century, bloodletting—carried out by physicians and barbers—was the most common medical intervention. An excess of blood was blamed for a range of symptoms, including fever and headache. Rather than cure people, however, the procedure carried risks of infection and hemorrhaging. Bizarrely, there may be a benefit to getting rid of some blood: it removes excess iron. For some people, too much iron carries a risk of heart disease and stroke. In 2008, a study showed that people who regularly give blood were at a reduced risk of developing these conditions.

A man, sitting on a bench, is having his right arm bled; the surgeon is applying the lancet, and an assistant is ready with a bowl.

WRISTY BUSINESS

Make a tight fist and hold your fist palm side up and you may be able to see a strange half-muscle, half-tendon, called the palmaris longus. It will be standing proud of the middle of your wrist, unless you are among the one in seven people who do not have one. This is not a problem: the palmaris longus is an evolutionary leftover that is found in nearly all other mammals, but has no known function in humans.

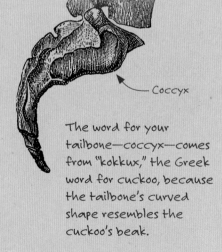

Coccyx

The word for your tailbone—coccyx—comes from "kokkux," the Greek word for cuckoo, because the tailbone's curved shape resembles the cuckoo's beak.

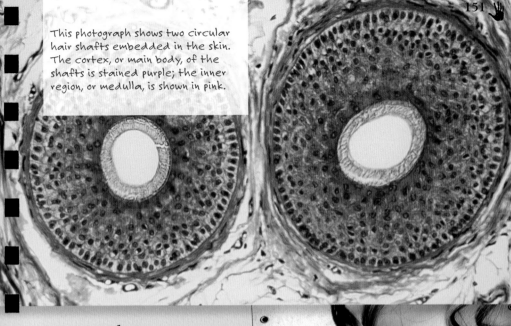

This photograph shows two circular hair shafts embedded in the skin. The cortex, or main body, of the shafts is stained purple; the inner region, or medulla, is shown in pink.

Hair today ...

The average diameter of individual human hairs is about 80 microns—just less than 0.1 mm. Most of that diameter is accounted for by the cortex, which is composed of dead cells, the protein keratin, globules of pigment, and some air spaces. It is the cortex that gives hair its strength and elasticity. Inside the cortex is a space called the medulla; in most hair it is empty, but in coarser hair, it is partially filled with soft, spongy tissue.

Outside the cortex is the cuticle, a protective covering made of flattened, dead keratin-rich cells arranged like overlapping roofing tiles. You can feel them: hold a hair near its root with one hand and slide two fingers of the other hand along the hair, away from the root—it should feel smooth. Repeat, but this time from the other end of the hair. Now, your fingers will catch on the tiny tiles, and the hair will feel rough.

... GONE TOMORROW
Strands of hair from Che Guevara (died 1967) were sold by a former CIA operative for $119,000 at auction in 2007, in Dallas, Texas. Other famous people whose hair has been sold after their death include Napoleon, Abraham Lincoln, Albert Einstein, John F. Kennedy, Marilyn Monroe, and Elvis Presley.

All gummed up?

If you were told as a child not to swallow chewing gum because it will stay in your stomach for years, you were misled. Chewing gum is mainly indigestible, but like (almost) any other indigestible matter you swallow, gum will pass right through you within a day or two.

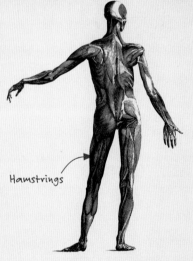

Hamstrings

HAM IT UP

The word "hamstring" can be used to refer to any of the muscles and tendons on the back of the thigh. It is derived from an Old English word "hamm," which means the back of the knee. The foodstuff we call ham is cured meat taken from the thighs of pigs.

The world's biggest collection of belly-button fluff, or "navel lint," is that of Graham Barker, from Western Australia. He began collecting in 1984.

Celebrity body part insurance

In 2006, American singer Mariah Carey insured her legs for $1 billion. In 2009, Formula One racing driver Fernando Alonso insured his thumbs for $13 million. Many other stories of celebrities insuring parts of their bodies have little or no basis in truth—for example, despite widespread reports, British singer Tom Jones did not insure his chest hair for $7 million, and Jennifer Lopez flatly denied insuring her bottom for $1 billion.

The phrase "all fingers and thumbs," meaning clumsy, was originally "all thumbs"—which makes much more sense. The change to the current version seems to have taken place in the late 19th century.

SEEING RED

Sunburn is an example of erythema—a blushing redness in the skin caused by extra blood flow in the capillaries in the skin. The word erythema comes from the Greek word *erythainein*, meaning "to become red." The increased blood flow brings oxygen, white blood cells, and antioxidants, to effect repair of the tissues and to prevent further damage. Erythema can also occur as a result of suction on the skin. A mild hickey is an example of this. Other causes of erythema include:

☞ Burns, including sunburn

☞ Infection and some diseases, including lupus and gout

☞ Massage or abrasion

☞ Dermatitis and psoriasis

☞ Exercise

☞ Chilblains

☞ Radiation treatment

A sunburned surfer

Don't blame me. I think my skin looks lovely.

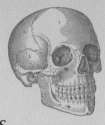

Wart are you worried about?

Warts are caused by members of the human papilloma virus (HPV) family. Some viruses in this family represent the biggest single cause of cervical cancer—but those that cause warts are not cancer-causing. The name "papilloma" comes from the word "papilla," which means a nipple-like protruberance. When HPV infects the skin, it causes cells in the outermost layer to proliferate. HPV can infect only humans, so you can't catch warts from other animals—even toads.

DEM BONES

The joints between bones can be:

- **Cartilaginous:** Connected by cartilage. Example: the disks between vertebrae.
- **Fibrous:** Connected by collagen-rich fibers. Example: sutures between the bones of the skull.
- **Synovial:** Not in contact, but surrounded by a fluid-filled membrane sac. Example: knee joint.

THE ZONULE OF ZINN
Not a location in a science fiction story, but a ring of fibers that connects the lens of the eye to the surrounding tissue, the zonule of Zinn is named after German anatomist and botanist Johann Gottfried Zinn (1727–1759). He also gave his name to the zinnia flower.

Zinnias

The first vertebra, which directly supports the skull at the top of the spine, is called the atlas.

WEB OF LIES

It is a commonly held belief that people swallow a total of four spiders per year in their sleep. Fortunately, the actual figure is probably zero. In order to swallow a spider in your sleep, you would have to be sleeping with your mouth open; you would most likely feel a spider crawling on your face and would wake up or close your mouth; if a spider made it into your mouth, you would almost certainly spit it out.

OUT OF BODY EXPERIENCE

In 2010, a human heart was kept alive outside the body for nearly 12 hours, thanks to a device called the Portable Organ Preservation System, which supplied it with warm, nutrient- and oxygen-rich blood. Previously, the same device kept a kidney alive—and making urine—for nearly 24 hours. The device is currently used only for research purposes but holds promise for use in transplant surgery.

I've got a bone called a sternum? You're ribbing me.

Rib cage

There are twelve pairs of ribs, each one attached to a different vertebra in the spine. The upper seven pairs are called "true ribs" and are joined to the sternum, or breastbone, by cartilage. The next three pairs are "false ribs" and are not joined to the sternum, but each is joined to the rib above it by cartilage. The final two pairs are "floating ribs"— they are not attached to the sternum at all.

There are about 50 meibomian glands on the inside of each of your upper eyelids that secrete an oily liquid called meibum, and about 25 more on the inside of each lower lid. Meibum stops the eyeball from drying out. It also prevents tears from spilling onto the cheek.

HOLDING ONTO YOUR TEETH

Teeth are not cemented into the bone of the jaw: they are connected by thousands of tiny fibers collectively known as the periodontal ligament. Similarly, the teeth are held firmly to the gums by thousands of tiny strands of connective tissue called gingival fibers.

ORGANS WE HAVE PAIRS OF …

All major organs except the following exist singly:

- Eyes
- Ears
- Kidneys
- Lungs
- Ovaries/testes

BONES WE HAVE ONLY ONE OF …

All bones except those listed here come in pairs:

- Sternum
- Pelvis
- Hyoid bone (supports the tongue)
- Mandible (lower jaw)
- Frontal and occipital bones of the skull
- Sphenoid bone (behind the eyes)
- Ethmoid bone (roof of the nose)
- Vomer bone (in the nose)
- Each vertebra in the spine

By the age of 70, the average human being will have produced:
- About 10,500 gallons (40,000 liters) of urine—enough to fill 500 bathtubs
- About ten tons of feces (9,000 kg)—equal to the weight of two adult elephants

Hair color

Human hair contains three types of melanin: ordinary brown melanin, darker brown eumelanin, and pinkish-red pheomelanin. The mixture of these three pigments determines hair color and is itself determined by genes. In red (ginger) hair, pheomelanin dominates; blond hair has low levels of eumelanin; black hair has high levels of eumelanin, while brown and auburn hair contains fairly equal proportions of all three pigments. People's hair turns gray or white as they age because melanin-producing cells in the hair follicle stop producing melanin, so that hairs grow out free of pigment.

Give up when you are a head

Guillotine

Many thousands of people have died by being decapitated, either in an execution or an accident. There are many reports of the severed head remaining conscious for several seconds. The most famous example was that of French scientist—and murderer—Henri Languille, who was executed on the guillotine in Orleans, France, in 1905. One of the spectators, a Dr. Beaurieux, gave an account of what happened immediately after Languille's head was severed from his body:

"I called in a strong, sharp voice: 'Languille!' I saw the eyelids slowly lift up, without any spasmodic contractions … but with an even movement, quite distinct and normal, such as happens in everyday life, with people awakened or torn from their thoughts. Next Languille's eyes very definitely fixed themselves on mine and the pupils focused themselves. I was not, then, dealing with the sort of vague dull look without any expression, that can be observed any day in dying people to whom one speaks: I was dealing with undeniably living eyes which were looking at me … I called out again and, once more, without any spasm, slowly, the eyelids lifted and undeniably living eyes fixed themselves on mine with perhaps even more penetration than the first time. There was a further closing of the eyelids, but now less complete. I attempted the effect of a third call; there was no further movement—and the eyes took on the glazed look which they have in the dead … The whole thing had lasted twenty-five to thirty seconds."

THERE IS A LATIN NAME FOR EVERY PART OF THE BODY, AND THE BODY ITSELF IS CALLED THE "CORPUS."

It takes about seven seconds for food to reach your stomach, via your esophagus, after swallowing.

> **Our bodies are our gardens—our wills are our gardeners.**
>
> William Shakespeare

The fish tapeworm's body consists of a chain of segments. In the center of each, eggs can be seen.

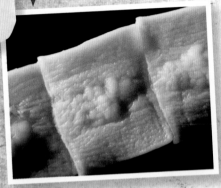

YOUR INNER TENNIS COURT

In the lungs, oxygen enters the blood from the air inside tiny hollow sacs called alveoli. There are around 240 million alveoli, and 1,250 miles (2,000 km) of capillaries, in each lung. All the alveoli in both lungs present a huge surface area. It is impossible to calculate the area accurately, because of the "fractal" nature of lungs: the closer you look, the more area you can see. Figures given in textbooks are typically in the range 540–4,300 square feet (50–400 sq m). Studies using an ordinary microscope in the 1970s estimated the total surface area for both lungs as up to 1,720 square feet (160 sq m); but studies in the 1980s looked more closely, with an electron microscope, and the estimate became 2,800 square feet (260 sq m)—approximately the size of a tennis court.

Worming its way in

The longest species of tapeworm that can make its home in the human digestive system is *Diphyllobothrium latum*, known as the fish tapeworm. These parasites can find their way into humans in raw or undercooked fish. The adults can grow to 30 feet (10 m) long. Like all tapeworms, these nasty creatures use tentacles on their heads as suction cups to hold onto the inside lining of the intestines—and they produce up to a million eggs every day.

Seeing with your brain

Believe it or not, the squares marked A and B in the image on the left, above, are exactly the same shade of gray—check the picture on the right to convince yourself. American cognitive scientist Edward Adelson, who created this illusion, explains that it "demonstrates the success rather than the failure of the visual system." Your brain creates an internal picture of reality, based on its experience and understanding of the world, rather than simply presenting you with exactly what your eyes see.

A POKE IN THE EYE

Cataract surgery has been performed for at least 2,700 years: writing in the 6th century BCE, Indian surgeon Susruta was the first to describe in detail a procedure that became known as couching, in which the cataract is pushed into the eye with a fine, blunt needle. A person can still see without a lens, albeit with only fixed focus—and the operation was a success, despite the inevitably high rate of complications. Couching—from the French *coucher*, meaning to lie down, remained the standard treatment for cataracts until the 18th century. From then on, the lens was removed from the eye, not simply pushed inside it. Modern ophthalmic surgeons still remove the lens, but they replace it with an artificial one.

Couching in 16th-century Germany. Note the assistant holding the patient's head steady.

Stroke a newborn baby's palm and his or her hand will close around your finger. This "palmar" reflex action disappears after about six months, as babies gain more conscious muscle control.

Why am I so fast? Because I'm a runner bean.

The dangly thing at the back of your throat is called the uvula, which is Latin for "little grape." It makes for one of the most unusual—and surely one of the most uncomfortable—places to have a piercing. The first uvula piercing took place in 1994. (Note: however it is portrayed in cartoons, the uvula does not actually vibrate when people sing.)

Meat-free achievements

American athlete Carl Lewis, voted Sportsman of the 20th Century by the International Olympic Committee after dominating sprint and long jump events and winning nine gold medals, was vegan for most of his sporting career.

The Christmas factor

Hemophilia B is a rare form of the blood-clotting disorder hemophilia. It is also called Christmas disease, after Steven Christmas, who, in 1952, was the first patient diagnosed with the condition. Christmas was found to be deficient in a blood-clotting compound called factor IX, which is often referred to as Christmas factor in his honor. Genetic studies of the Russian royal family have revealed that they, too, suffered from the same rare form of hemophilia.

Nicholas II of Russia with his family (left to right): Olga, Maria, Nicholas II, Alexandra Fyodorovna, Anastasia, Alexei, and Tatiana.

All male primates except male humans have a bone in the penis, called a baculum.

Varicose veins on a man's leg

YOU'RE SO VEIN

Canadian physician William Osler (1849–1919) once wrote, "Varicose veins are the result of an improper selection of grandparents." The risk of developing varicose veins is partly inherited—via a mutated gene called FOXC2 on chromosome 16. But anyone can develop the condition. The greatest risk factors are prolonged standing, obesity, and pregnancy. Varicose veins are the result of a buildup of blood in the veins, typically in the lower legs, which makes the veins swell.

GRIM TROPHY
Shrunken heads were war trophies made until the mid-20th century in some parts of South America and certain islands in the western Pacific Ocean. They were made from real heads of people killed in battles or raids.

The breast dishes on the menu ...

❦ In 2011, American singer-songwriter Lady Gaga began court action against an ice-cream parlor in London after it began selling an ice cream called "Baby Gaga," which was made from human milk. Previously, the product had been removed from sale while local food standards officials tested it to make sure it was safe for "human consumption."

❦ In 2010, a New York chef posted a recipe for breast milk cheese on his blog, and invited people to come to his restaurant and try the cheese while supplies lasted. He had the idea after his family's freezer had become overstocked with milk expressed by his wife.

❦ In 2008, a restaurateur in Switzerland gave up on his plan to serve dishes made with breast milk, after local authorities threatened him with lawsuits. One of the dishes he had created was "antelope steak with chanterelle sauce spiked with cognac and breast milk."

Spinach

Spinach is good for you, but not as good for you as you may think. It is high in fiber and is an excellent source of many vitamins. It is also rich in iron and calcium—but it contains a compound that hampers the availability of these important minerals: oxalic acid (vitamin B9). In the digestive system, the oxalic acid binds to the iron to form iron oxalate and with the calcium to make calcium oxalate; the body cannot use either of these compounds, and only a small proportion of the iron and calcium is absorbed.

If you're going to be a level III, you may as well go the whole hog!

TO BALDLY GO

Men tend to lose hair as they age along the temples, while women's hair thins out all over. Male pattern baldness is caused by male hormones (androgens) and is called androgenic alopecia; it is graded using the Hamilton-Norwood Scale, according to its severity, from level I to level VII.

The flap of skin that joins the underside of your tongue to the bottom of your jaw is called the frenulum—or, more properly, the frenulum linguae. The word "frenulum" is Latin and means "little bridle." There is also a frenulum between your upper lip and your gums (frenulum labii superioris) and another between your lower lip and your gums (frenulum labii inferioris), which you can easily feel with the tip of your tongue.

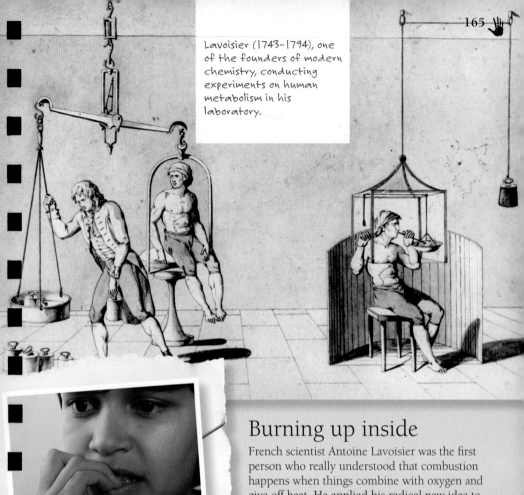

Lavoisier (1743-1794), one of the founders of modern chemistry, conducting experiments on human metabolism in his laboratory.

NASTY HABITS
The scientific term for eating your own boogers is automucophagy. The scientific term for biting your fingernails is onychophagia.

Burning up inside

French scientist Antoine Lavoisier was the first person who really understood that combustion happens when things combine with oxygen and give off heat. He applied his radical new idea to the human body and realized that body heat is generated by combustion of carbohydrates from food, fueled by oxygen from the air. He carried out dozens of careful experiments, painstakingly weighing people, taking their temperature, and measuring the amount of oxygen they consumed when at rest, after food, and after exercise. He had founded the modern science of metabolism and exercise physiology—but he was beheaded nevertheless, during the French Revolution, aged just 51.

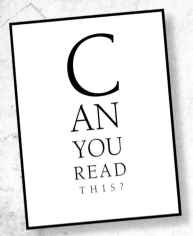

C
AN
YOU
READ
THIS?

When taking a sight test, people are made to stand 20 feet (6 m) away from a chart on the wall. Their overall visual acuity is often given as a fraction, based on what a "normal" person would be able to make out at 20 feet. So, 20/20 vision describes "normal" vision—in other words, the person being tested sees as well at 20 feet as a "normal" person would see at the same distance. Someone with outstanding visual acuity might have 20/10 vision: they can see at 20 feet as well as a normal person can see at 10 feet.

YOUR BODY DOESN'T NEED ...

There are some metallic elements that your body most certainly does not need—they are toxic, even in small amounts. And, because they are not involved in the body's chemical processes, they are not easily excreted and can build up in your tissues.

- Lead
- Mercury
- Uranium
- Arsenic
- Cadmium
- Beryllium
- Antimony

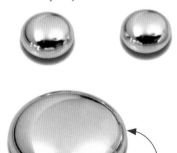

Mercury drops

Laser eye surgery

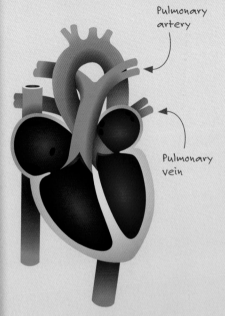

Pulmonary
artery

Pulmonary
vein

SHINE A LIGHT

1961: The first medical use of lasers was the removal of a tattoo, by American dermatologist Leon Goldman, at the University of Cincinnati. (*Laser used:* ruby.)

1961: The first use of lasers in the eye, for "photocoagulation" of a patient's retina, performed by American ophthalmologist Charles J. Campbell at Columbia University. (*Laser used:* ruby.)

1967: The introduction of bloodless laser surgery, cutting through skin and other tissue with a "laser scalpel," at the American Optical Corporation, Massachusetts. (*Laser used:* CO2.)

1987: The first use of lasers to modify the shape of the cornea, in order to correct vision, using a procedure called LASIK (laser-assisted in situ keratomileusis), carried out by Marguerite B. MacDonald at Tulane University, New Orleans. (*Laser used*: UV excimer.)

1989: The first use of lasers in dentistry, by American dentist Terry Myers, in Detroit, Michigan. (*Laser used:* Nd:YAG.)

All arteries carry blood away from the heart; all veins carry blood back to the heart. All arteries carry oxygenated blood—except one: the pulmonary artery, through which deoxygenated blood is pushed toward the lungs. Similarly, there is only one vein that carries oxygenated blood: the pulmonary vein carries blood from the lungs back to the heart.

THE SCIENTIFIC TERM FOR BELCHING IS "ERUCTATION."

Big feet

The word "sciapodous" means "having large feet." The word comes from an ancient Greek legend of the Sciapodes—small creatures with one large foot. The world's biggest feet—not including those that belong to people with diseases such as elephantiasis—belonged to American actor Matthew McGrory (1973–2005). Standing 7 feet 6 inches (2.29 m) tall, McGrory was often cast as a "giant"—including his role in the film *Big Fish*. He wore size 29½ shoes—and his big toes alone were said to be about 4 inches (10 cm) long.

I don't get why I only have 1 foot. It's at least 2 feet long!

This illustration of a monopod (person with one foot) is from the Nuremburg Chronicle, dated 1493.

Wake up and smell the medicine!

TAKE THE PAIN AWAY

Some headache remedies contain caffeine (look at the label, it is true). One of the effects of caffeine is to reduce blood flow to the head by constricting arteries in the neck. It also helps your body to absorb other active ingredients in headache remedies more quickly.

WHAT IS THIS?

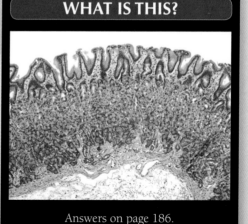

Answers on page 186.

A plaque in memory of Alois Alzheimer.

Forgetfulness disease

In 1901, 51-year-old Auguste Deter was admitted to the Institution for the Mentally Ill and Epileptics, in Frankfurt, Germany, after she had been showing increasing signs of dementia. During interviews with one of the doctors there, Deter repeatedly stated, "I seem to have lost myself." The doctor called her symptoms Forgetfulness Disease. After her death in 1906, he found amyloid plaques (protein deposits) in her brain. The doctor's name was Alois Alzheimer, and the disease he diagnosed is now known as Alzheimer's disease.

Around 10% of people are left-handed.

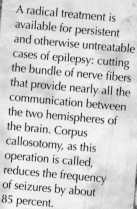

A radical treatment is available for persistent and otherwise untreatable cases of epilepsy: cutting the bundle of nerve fibers that provide nearly all the communication between the two hemispheres of the brain. Corpus callosotomy, as this operation is called, reduces the frequency of seizures by about 85 percent.

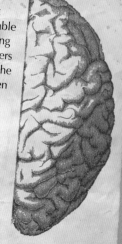

One person's waste, another's treatment

A new and slightly disturbing treatment developed by a team of doctors in Australia has proven very successful in dealing with inflammation of the colon caused by the bacterium *Clostridium difficile*. Known as fecal transplant, the treatment involves extracting bacteria from the stools of another person, ideally a relative, then depositing those bacteria into the patient's colon. The "transplant" can be effected via a series of enemas or through a gastric tube that enters at the patient's nose and passes down the throat and into the stomach. The treatment restores the natural balance of gut bacteria, keeping the population of *C. difficile* at bay.

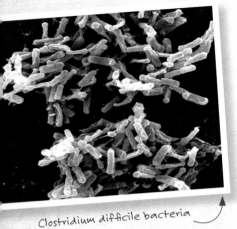

Clostridium difficile bacteria

THE ROLE OF OXYTOCIN IN A BABY'S LIFE …

- The orgasm that is usually part of the process of creating a baby raises the level of the hormone oxytocin in the blood; oxytocin promotes feelings of attachment and has a role in sex and family bonding.

- During labor, oxytocin in the mother stimulates the uterus to contract, pushing out the baby. The hormone also stimulates bonding between mother and baby.

- After the baby has been born, oxytocin once again makes the uterus contract, to expel the placenta. Midwives often give extra oxytocin, injected into the woman's thigh, to speed this process up.

- After the birth, the baby's sucking on the nipple causes the hypothalamus to produce oxytocin, which stimulates the woman's breasts to release milk—this is called the "let-down reflex."

The end of decay?

In 2010, researchers at University of Groningen, in the Netherlands, worked out the structure and modus operandi of an enzyme called glucansucrase, which makes plaque stick to teeth. Plaque is the film of bacteria that causes tooth decay and gum disease. If scientists can find substances that inhibit the action of glucansucrase and add those substances to toothpaste, or even foods, tooth decay might be eradicated.

SHELL-BEING

Drinking snail juice formed by cutting or impaling snails above a bowl was a traditional remedy for coughs in many countries for hundreds of years. It was also used to treat gout, whitlow, boils, eczema, and kidney stones. In France in the 19th century, snails were dried, crushed, and added to cough lozenges. As recently as 2010, over-enthusiastic religious leader Charles Stewart, of Hialeah, Florida, made his followers drink the juice of freshly cut snails—sadly, most of his patients became ill.

I'm sure that's not a cough. It's probably a frog in your throat.

Common garden snail

YOUR BODY NEEDS ...

... molybdenum

It is perhaps the least-known essential mineral, but you cannot live without molybdenum. This metallic element is involved in some fundamental enzyme reactions. Fortunately, the body needs only tiny amounts of molybdenum: an adult needs a little more than a millionth of an ounce (45 micrograms) per day, a child even less. Molybdenum is found in legumes (peas, beans, and lentils), nuts, and whole grains—studies show that average daily intake is comfortably above the recommended minimum.

Peas contain molybdenum

Toothpaste

Worth a try

Reportedly the most successful home treatment for bee stings is toothpaste. Dabbing a little toothpaste onto the affected area can soothe pain for hours. One often-quoted reason for the effect is that toothpaste is alkaline and bee stings are acidic. While this is true, it almost certainly has no bearing on the success of this treatment, because the acidic sting is encapsulated underneath the epidermis, so that little toothpaste can reach it, and the pain of a bee sting is due to a venom, not its acidity. Instead, the toothpaste creates a tingling and cooling sensation that simulates the relief felt by scratching, but without the damaging effect of scratching—namely, prolonging the inflammation, damaging tissues, and increasing the risk of infection.

The protein collagen is a major constituent of connective tissue and bones. Its name literally means "glue maker," because glue can be made from boiled bones—and the sticky part is the boiled collagen.

A SPORTING GUIDE TO THE MASSES OF THE MAJOR ORGANS IN AN ADULT …

- ♥ **Eye ball**: 1 ounce (25 g)
- ● **Tennis ball**: 2 ounces (58 g)
- ♥ **Kidneys**: 5 ounces (140 g) each
- ● **Pool ball**: 5½ ounces (160 g)
- ♥ **Stomach (empty)**: 6 ounces (170 g)
- ♥ **Spleen**: 6 ounces (170 g)
- ♥ **Heart**: 11 ounces (300 g)
- ● **Soccer ball**: 1 pound (450 g)
- ♥ **Lungs**: 1 pound (450 g) each
- ● **Basketball**: 1 pound 6 ounces (624 g)
- ♥ **Brain**: 3 pounds (1.35 kg)
- ♥ **Liver**: 3 pounds 3 ounces (1.45 kg)
- ● **Lightest-allowed bowling ball**: 6 pounds (2.7 kg)
- ♥ **Skin**: 9 pounds (4 kg)

[NOTE: averaged between men and women, and across adult ages]

Colored scanning electron micrograph (SEM) of cilia covering the epithelial lining of the nasal cavity.

About 1 in 10,000 babies is born with their major organs reversed left-to-right, so that, for example, the heart is slightly to right of center. This condition is called situs invertus.

Frantic activity in your nose and throat

The tiny hairlike structures, called cilia, on the mucous lining inside your nose flick to-and-fro a steady 15 times per second. The movement is similar to that of a windshield wiper—a rapid, forceful push and a more relaxed drawing back. This regular pulsing motion pushes dust- and bacteria-laden mucus down to the top of your throat, so that it can be swallowed. The same ciliated lining is present in the windpipe, but in this case, the cilia push the mucus upward—again, so that it can be swallowed. If the cilia in the windpipe are damaged—for example, through smoking—then the only way to get rid of the mucus is to cough.

Left side of nose

Right side of nose

View from left eye

View from right eye

Binocular view

BOTH EYES OPEN

Having two eyes, or binocular vision, gives you the ability to perceive depth by seeing in three dimensions. But it is also vital in being able to look to the sides without turning your head. Close your right eye and look to the right with your left eye; you will find that your nose almost completely blocks your view.

The mammary glands, which produce milk in a lactating woman's breasts, are actually a type of sweat gland. Like all sweat glands, they are lined with a layer of muscle cells, which squeeze out their secretion.

Artificial stomach

In 2006, scientists at the Institute of Food Research in Norwich, U.K., built an artificial stomach, in order to study the process of digestion. The "Dynamic Gastric Model," about the size of a large microwave oven, very closely simulates the physical and chemical environment of the human stomach and small intestine. It injects enzymes at the right time and mixes the food using the same forces a real stomach uses. The scientist in charge of the project, Dr. Martin Wickham, was reported as saying "It's so realistic, it can even vomit."

A plate from the Egyptian "Book of the Dead," showing the weighing of the heart in the underworld.

I'm white.
I'm a lily.
But, I have no liver.

A balanced personality?

During the mummification process, the ancient Egyptians removed the internal organs from the body. The only major organ they returned to the body was the heart, which they believed held wisdom and knowledge—although first, they would hold a symbolic ritual, in which the heart was weighed on a huge pair of scales, against the feather of Maat, which symbolized justice.

An adult human body contains about $^1/_{10}$ ounce (3 g) of fluorine, mostly in bones and teeth. This is about the same amount of fluorine as is found (as fluoride ions) in 25 standard-size packs of fluoride toothpaste.

From the Middle Ages, the liver was seen as the seat of courage. The term "lily-livered," meaning cowardly, comes from the idea that an uncourageous person would have no blood in their liver, which would then be white, like a lily. Shakespeare used the term in "Macbeth" and "King Lear." And in another of his plays, "Twelfth Night," Shakespeare wrote: "... you find so much blood in his liver as will clog the foot of a flea ...."

Listening in

The first stethoscope was created on the spur of the moment in 1816, by a shy young French doctor called René Laennec. People had been listening to the beating heart, by placing their ear directly onto a patient's chest, for thousands of years—at least since the time of Greek physician Hippocrates in the 5th century BCE. But Laennec was too embarrassed to do this to a female patient, so he rolled a wad of paper into a tube. He was so impressed with how his impromptu device amplified the sound of the woman's heart that he designed a wooden version based on the ear trumpet, used at the time by the hard of hearing. The binaural (two-ear) stethoscope was invented in 1851, by Irish doctor Arthur Leared.

Laennec examines a consumptive patient using a stethoscope in front of his students at the Necker Hospital, Paris, France.

I got a convertible so I could even out my liver spots.

SUN SPOTS

The blemishes on aging skin, known as liver spots, have nothing to do with the liver. They are caused by prolonged exposure to the ultraviolet radiation in sunlight. The ultraviolet causes damage to the skin, and in response, the body overproduces the skin pigment melanin. The damage also causes a yellow-brown pigment called lipofuscin to accumulate. In frequent drivers of left-hand drive cars, liver spots tend to be more common on the left side of the face and left arm—the side that receives more exposure to sunlight. In countries with right-hand drive cars liver spots tend to be more common on the right side of the face and right arm.

A QUESTION OF DEGREES

♥ **First-degree burn** (superficial thickness): Superficial damage to the epidermis (top layer of skin) and some redness, which disappears temporarily if you press on the skin. Heals in a few days.

♥ **Second-degree burn** (partial thickness): Dermis also damaged, with swelling and redness; a second-degree burn typically produces blisters. May leave a scar. Heals in two to three weeks.

♥ **Third-degree burn** (full thickness): Epidermis and dermis largely destroyed, with damage to subcutaneous (under-skin) tissue and destruction of hair roots. In severe cases, muscles, tendons, and even bone may be destroyed.

THAT GIRL HAS POTENTIAL
A baby girl is born with about 60,000 immature egg cells, called oocytes, in her ovaries. Although every one of these cells has the potential to do so, only a few hundred will mature and be released during the woman's reproductive lifetime.

Tasting with your lungs

In 2010, researchers at the University of Maryland were surprised to find taste receptors … in human lungs. They were even more surprised to find that these receptors respond to bitter substances, by opening the small airways into the lungs—the bronchioles. The shortness of breath associated with asthma is caused by these airways becoming constricted as muscles that surround them tense up. The researchers found that bitter substances cause the new-found receptors to send signals to the muscles, causing them to relax. The response was faster than that to the standard "bronchodilator" treatment given to asthma sufferers, which has the same effect. The discovery holds the promise of future drugs containing bitter compounds that will bring better and faster relief.

I've got the most terrible cold. Honestly!

Starve a fever?
Feed a cold?

The old saying, "Starve a fever, feed a cold," has its origins in at least the 16th century. It is clearly inconsistent at best, since fever is often a symptom of a cold—but is there any truth in it? The saying evolved in two phases. Firstly, the fever: as far back as the ancient Greeks, some people had considered food as a fuel that burns, and so adding food to an already hot body seemed to them like throwing wood onto a fire that was already out of control. However, the first time the specific advice to stop eating in response to fever appeared was the 16th century, and by the 19th century, it was largely accepted as fact. At that time, people believed that colds were accompanied by a drop in body temperature—and so the saying was complete. However, there is nothing to be gained in overeating for a cold nor in fasting for a fever. A fever is part of your body's response to infection, and with any infection, your body needs a good, balanced diet to help in its battle.

ROLL CALL

Tongue rolling is often given as an example of simple genetics—even in some textbooks. It is often said that people can either roll their tongue or not, and that this ability is determined by a single gene. However, this is not true: two non-tongue-rolling parents can have a tongue-rolling child, and many people can learn to roll their tongue; and different people can roll their tongues by different amounts.

WRONG NAME?

The word "thyroid" comes from the ancient Greek word *qyreoeidh*, which means "large, oblong shield." Perhaps it would have been better to call it the psychoid, from the ancient Greek word for butterfly—*psyche*—since the thyroid gland is clearly shaped much more like a butterfly than a large shield.

Ooooops! No more soda for me!

Whoopee cushion

Airs and graces

A belch is mostly made up of air that has been swallowed during eating and therefore consists mostly of nitrogen and oxygen. Belches caused by drinking fizzy (carbonated) drinks will also contain a good deal of carbon dioxide, the gas in those bubbles. Flatus—the gas released at the other end—typically has a very different composition: while it is still mostly nitrogen, much of the oxygen has been absorbed by the body or used by aerobic bacteria in the gut. The products of those bacteria vary but are typically hydrogen and carbon dioxide. The smell of flatus comes from pungent sulfur-containing compounds also produced by gut bacteria.

> And I thought I was the biggest hair ball in the world!

Giant hair ball

Hair balls do not only affect cats. Some people who engage in trichophagia (hair eating) end up with large hair balls in their stomach. The most incredible case was of an 18-year-old woman who had been complaining of stomach pain and frequent vomiting, and who had lost more than 40 pounds (18 kg) in weight in just a few months. In 2007, surgeons at the Rush University Medical Center in Chicago, Illinois, removed a 10-pound (4.5-kg) hair ball that had been taking up almost all the available space in the woman's stomach.

THE LAST LAUGH

☺ A 1989 study in the U.S.A. found that laughter reduces all the indicators of stress, including the main stress hormone, cortisol.

☺ A 2010 study in Japan found that "mirthful laughter elicited by comic movies induces beneficial vascular function"—in other words, laughing is good for your heart and blood circulation. Blood pressure and heart rate went up, but blood vessels became more elastic, or "compliant."

☺ A 2006 study by American scientists found that just the expectation of mirthful laughter increased the concentration of endorphins in the blood by 27 percent and human growth hormone (HGH) by 87 percent. These compounds "carry important, positive implications for wellness, disease-prevention and most certainly stress-reduction."

The sinoatrial node receives a signal from the brain to start a contraction.

This signal gets passed to the atrioventricular node, which spreads the signal from the atria (the upper chambers of the heart) to the ventricles (the lower chambers).

Your continued existence depends upon many parts of your body, but few more than the sinoatrial node. This group of cells is the body's natural pacemaker, producing regular electric pulses that orchestrate all your heart's electrical activity. Discovered in 1907, this group of cells, measuring just 0.4 × 0.1 inches (10 by 3 mm), is built into the right atrium at the top of the heart.

ARE YOU RECEIVING?

Your brain would be pretty useless without input from sensors, or receptors, that feed it information. There are receptors throughout the body (interoceptors) that provide information on internal conditions, such as the concentration of dissolved chemicals, amounts of fluids, or the stretching of particular organs. We are normally unaware of this kind of feedback. Receptors that send information about what is going on outside your body are called exteroceptors. They include receptors for the five senses, but there are also receptors for pain (nociceptors) and temperature (thermoceptors). Your brain also processes information about your position in space and the relative position of different parts of your body, sent by proprioceptors.

NASA astronaut Bruce McCandless processing data from his proprioceptors about his position in space.

Y the difference?

The 23 pairs of chromosomes in human cells include a pair of sex chromosomes. Women's cells have a pair of the same kind, the X chromosome. Men's cells have one X chromosome and one Y, and so it is in the Y chromosome that differences between women and men must lie—and it has only 78 active genes, compared to about 2,000 genes on the X chromosome. One of the most important is called SRY (Sex-determining Region of the Y chromosome). It is this gene that forces gonads in the human embryo to become masculinized into testes, and thereby starts a chain of events that will last a lifetime.

The average human brain has shrunk by about the size of a tennis ball over the past 20,000 years.

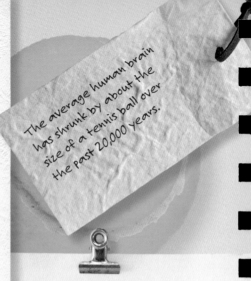

Soviet stamp with the head of Lenin

I know Y!

Yes, and I know U!

The body of Russian revolutionary leader Lenin was embalmed after his death in 1924, by immersing it in a bath of glycerine and preservatives. The body has been on public display more or less continuously ever since, in a specially built mausoleum, where it is washed with glycerine every two weeks and given a bath once every 18 months. In 2011, two-thirds of 250,000 people in an online poll stated that they thought Lenin should now be buried.

Vitamin K

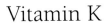

In most countries, midwives inject Vitamin K into a newborn baby or give oral doses of the vitamin over the baby's first month. Vitamin K is essential to the process of blood clotting; in most people, it is produced by helpful bacteria in the gut. But newborns' guts do not yet have these bacteria, and there are only tiny amounts of vitamin K in mother's milk and formula milk.

NOSE JOB
The earliest known rhinoplasty—reshaping of the nose—took place around 500 BCE. It was described, and practiced, by the influential Indian surgeon Sushruta, mostly to rebuild criminals' noses cut off as a punishment.

STUDYING THE BODY

The suffix "logy" refers to the study of something.

- **Adenology:** Study of glands
- **Allergology:** Allergies
- **Anesthesiology:** Anesthesia and anesthetics
- **Arthrology:** Joints
- **Audiology:** Hearing, especially impaired hearing
- **Cardiology:** The circulatory system, especially the heart
- **Chondrology:** Cartilage
- **Cytology:** Cells and cell function
- **Dermatology:** Skin
- **Desmopathology:** Diseases that affect the ligaments and tendons
- **Emetology:** Vomiting and its causes
- **Emmenology:** Menstruation and disorders of menstruation
- **Endocrinology:** Endocrine glands and their secretions (hormones)
- **Enterology:** The intestines
- **Epidemiology:** The frequency and distribution of diseases
- **Gastroenterology:** Diseases of the stomach and intestines
- **Gerontology:** The aging process
- **Gynecology:** The female reproductive system
- **Hematology:** Blood
- **Herniology:** Hernias

continued on page 184

continued from page 183

☞ **Histology:** The microscopic structure of body tissues

☞ **Hysterology:** Uterus

☞ **Immunology:** Immunity

☞ **Laryngology:** Larynx

☞ **Neonatology:** Newborns

☞ **Nephrology:** Kidneys

☞ **Neurology:** The nerves and nervous system

☞ **Neuropathology:** Diseases of the nervous system

☞ **Oncology:** Cancers

☞ **Ophthalmology:** Diseases of the eye

☞ **Osteology:** Bones and bone disorders

☞ **Pathology:** Disease

☞ **Pharmacology:** The actions of drugs

☞ **Physiology:** The functions of the body

☞ **Proctology:** Disorders of the rectum and anus

☞ **Psychopathology:** Mental diseases

☞ **Ptolaryngology:** Ear, nose, and throat

☞ **Radiology:** The use of various forms of radiation for diagnosis and therapy

☞ **Stomatology:** Diseases of the mouth

☞ **Syndesmology:** Ligaments

☞ **Tenology:** Tendons

☞ **Toxicology:** Poisons

☞ **Urology:** Diseases of the kidneys and the urinary tract

What a drag

It has long been known that smoking causes damage to DNA inside the body, and it is this damage that is responsible for smoking's link to various types of cancer. The main culprits are substances called polycyclic aromatic hydrocarbons (PAHs)—or rather their "metabolites" (secondary compounds produced by the body's attempts to deal with the PAHs). A 2010 study, carried out at the University of Minnesota, found that the concentration of these metabolites reaches its peak as soon as 15 minutes after finishing a cigarette.

WELL CONNECTED

Ligaments and tendons are very similar types of connective tissue; the main difference is that ligaments connect bone to bone, while tendons connect muscle to bone.

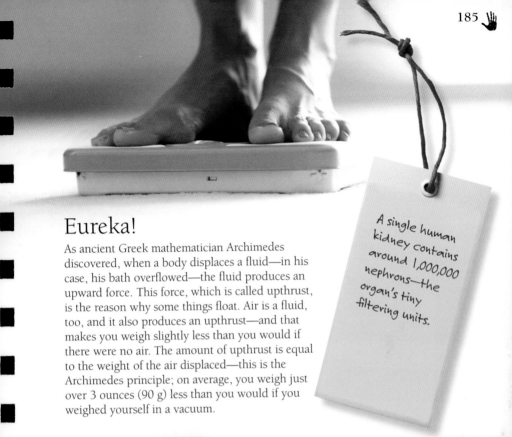

Eureka!

As ancient Greek mathematician Archimedes discovered, when a body displaces a fluid—in his case, his bath overflowed—the fluid produces an upward force. This force, which is called upthrust, is the reason why some things float. Air is a fluid, too, and it also produces an upthrust—and that makes you weigh slightly less than you would if there were no air. The amount of upthrust is equal to the weight of the air displaced—this is the Archimedes principle; on average, you weigh just over 3 ounces (90 g) less than you would if you weighed yourself in a vacuum.

A single human kidney contains around 1,000,000 nephrons—the organ's tiny filtering units.

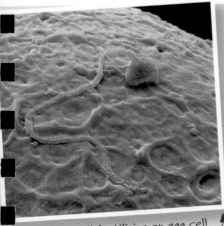

Sperm cell fertilizing an egg cell

COME OUT OF YOUR SHELL

There is a sugar-protein shell around every human egg, called the zona pellucida. Sperm cells attach to this shell easily and then have to face the daunting task of breaking through it. If one manages it, as soon as it does, the zona pellucida hardens, so that no more sperms can get through. The shell expands as the embryo divides inside it, until eventually a crack appears, and the embryo "hatches," allowing it to attach to the wall of the womb. After *in vitro* fertilization, the zona pellucida is often broken artificially, increasing the chance that an embryo will implant in the mother's womb.

WHAT IS THIS?
ANSWERS

In what follows, 'SEM' stands for scanning electron micrograph—a photograph taken through a scanning electron microscope.

Page	Answer
39	SEM showing macrophages, part of the body's natural defense system, attacking a cancer cell; injecting it with toxins. The cancer cell is the large object, the macrophages are the knobbly cells attached to it, and all around are red blood cells.
51	False-colored SEM showing single-celled *Salmonella typhimurium* bacteria (pink) invading human cells (yellow). These bacteria are the most common cause of salmonellosis, characterized by diarrhea, fever, and abdominal cramps.
65	Colored SEM of the surface of the human tongue. The pointed projections are called filiform papillae. They are the most common protuberance on the tongue's upper surface, and they are involved in detecting pressure rather than taste.
74	False-colored SEM of sensory hair cells from inside the cochlea. The inner ear is awash with a fluid called endolymph, and vibrations of sound waves detected by the eardrum pass through the fluid, making these hairs move to and fro. Each V-shaped arrangement sits atop a single cell.

94 False-colored SEM showing a bed bug (*Cimex lectularius*). Bed bugs inject their long mouthparts (colored lilac) through the skin to obtain the blood they need to survive.

125 Transmission electron micrograph of a section through a measles virus. Spread via fluids from the mouth or nose of an infected person, measles still causes more than 100,000 deaths per year worldwide, nearly all of them in developing countries, where the majority of people have limited access to vaccines.

138 Color-enhanced SEM showing clusters of bright orange methycillin-resistant *Staphylococcus aureus* (MRSA) bacteria. Each bacterium is about 19 millionths of an inch (0.0005 mm) in diameter.

168 Light micrograph of a thin section of human stomach lining, or "gastric mucosa." This pitted lining contains gland cells that produce gastric fluid, which includes concentrated hydrochloric acid.

Index

Credits

Key: b bottom; c center; l left; r right; t top

11cl Dover Books 11cr Dover Books 13c Dover Books 14tr Eric Erbe, digital colorization by Christopher Pooley, both of USDA, ARS, EMU 14bl Getty Images Barcroft Media 15tr Dover Books 15cl 15b Getty Images/George Gobet 20b Dover Books 21tr CDC 22bl NASA 22b NASA 26bl Dover Books 28tc Warut Roonguthai 31cr PD-ART 32tl Jörg Hempel 32br Getty Images/ Hulton Archive/Stringer 33l Image by Ute Frevert; false color by Margaret Shear 33bcl Lopez-Garcia, F., Zahn, R., Riek, R., Wuthrich, K. & RCSB 33bl CDC 34tl Science Photo Library/Eye of Science 34br Dover Books 37 Science Photo Library/ Gissels 39tr Susan Arnold 39bl Marie-Lan Nguyen 39tr Getty Images/ Jemal Countess 40tr Dover Books 43c Getty Images/Imagno 44tl Arthur Shuster & Arthur E. Shipley: Britain's Heritage of Science. London, 1917 44tr Dover Books 46tr Science Photo Library/Steve Gschmeissner 48c /1912 Catalogue General Antiquites Egyptiennes du Musée du Caire DT57.C2 vol 59 G. Elliot Smith 48tr César Landeros Soriano 49c Sven Rosborn 48bl South Tirol Museum 50bl University Tübingen Hilde Jensen 51tr Massachusetts Institute of Technology Patrick Gillooly 51br Rocky Mountain Laboratories, NIAID, NIH 53c Science Photo Library/Steve Gschmeissner 55b Wilhelm Conrad Röntgen 55bl Wilhelm Conrad Röntgen 56tr Science Photo Library/Medical Images, Universal Medical Group 57b emilio labrador 57tl Science Photo Library/Eye of Science 59bc Dover Books 60t Gilles San Martin 61tl Gilles San Martin 62tl jma.work 62bl Brady National Photographic Art Gallery (Washington, D.C.) 65bl NASA 65br Science Photo Library/Science Photo Library 68cl Dover Books 68c Dover Books 70tr Dover Books 72tl Library of Congress Prints and Photographs Division 72tr avlxyz 74tl Science Photo Library/ Steve Gschmeissner 75br Dover Books 77tr Dover Books 78tl Dover Books 78cr Dover Books 82bl Science Photo Library/ Dr. Richard Kessel & Dr. GeneE Shih, Visuals Unlimited 87tl Lucarelli 90tl Bridgeman Art Library Leicester Arts & Museums 93tr Ed Uthman, MD 93bl CDC Dr. Don Millar 94tr CDC Janice Haney Carr 98cl Science Photo Library/ Prof. P. Motta / G. Macchiarelli / University

"La Sapienza," Rome 99tr Gaetan Lee 101cr Jacques Donnez Jacques Donnez 102tr Science Photo Library/Manfred Kage 104tr Science Photo Library/Science Photo Library/ 104b Lange123 108tr Carlos Paris 109t http://www.nv.doe.gov 111tr Science Photo Library/Royal Observatory, Edinburgh 116tl Campana Collection/ Jastrow 118tl Pöllö 119l Science Photo Library/Science Photo Library/ 121tl John Fleagle 123 cr National Library of Medicine Visible Human Project 123br National Library of Medicine Visible Human Project 124cr CDC/Dr. Erskine Palmer/B.G. Partin 125br CDC Courtesy of Cynthia S. Goldsmith; William Bellini, PhD 127tl Science Photo Library/NYPL / Science Source 130 tl Dover Books 131t Science Photo Library/Martin Shields 131bl Dover Books 132tr Bugmore 133tr Dover Books 135cr Images from the History of Medicine (NLM) Antoni Baratti 137cr Dover Books 136br CDC Jeff Hageman, M.H.S./Janice Haney Carr 140br Science Photo Library/Sue Ford 142br Science Photo Library/Steve Gschmeissner 145t Science Photo Library/ Sheila Terry 146tr Dover Books 147b Images from the History of Medicine (NLM) George Cruikshank 148cr Clive Phillips-Wolley 150tl Images from the History of Medicine (NLM) Cintio d'Amato 150cr Hwilms 150cr Dover Books 151tr Science Photo Library/Astrid & Hanns-Frieder Michler 152cl Dover Books 152br Graham Barker 154tr Dover Books 156r Dover Books 159tr Science Photo Library/ CNRI 160t Edward H. Adelson 160br Images from the History of Medicine (NLM) Georg Bartisch 162tr Sasha l 163t Getty Images/Steve Bronstein 164b Getty Images/Science & Society Picture Library 168tr Michel Voglenray, Wilhelm Pleydenwurff 168br Nephron 169tr Bonio 169bc Dover Books 170tl Centers for Disease Control and Prevention/Marco Tolo 173t Charles Daghlian 175tl FinnBjo 176tr Théobald Chartran 182tr NASA 185bl Science Photo Library/Thierry Berrod, Mona Lisa Production

iStock, Shutterstock

While every effort has been made to credit copyright holders, Quarto would like to apologize should there have been any omissions or errors, and would be pleased to make the appropriate correction in future editions.